PATCHWORK SHOWCASE

Simple Quilts with Big Impact

NANCY MAHONEY

Martingale & COMPANY

Dedication

To Tom and Prince, who keep me on my toes!

Acknowledgments

I am most grateful to and appreciative of the following people and companies who have so generously given their support and products for the projects in this book:

- Mary Green, Editorial Director; Karen Soltys, Acquisitions and Development Editor; Terry Martin, Editorial Administrative Assistant; and the entire staff at Martingale & Company for their hard work
- Clothworks and David Peha
- P & B Textiles and Julie Scribner
- Timeless Treasures Fabrics Inc. and Emily Cohen
- American & Efird Inc. and Marci Brier for Mettler and Signature threads
- Hobbs Bonded Fibers and H.D. Wilbanks for batting
- Prym Dritz/Omnigrid for notions, rotary cutters, rulers, and mats
- Quilting Creations Inc. and Aaron Bell for quilting stencils
- The Electric Quilt Company for computer software

Credits

President: Nancy J. Martin
CEO: Daniel J. Martin
Publisher: Jane Hamada
Editorial Director: Mary V. Green
Managing Editor: Tina Cook
Technical Editor: Darra Williamson
Copy Editor: Durby Peterson
Design Director: Stan Green
Illustrator: Laurel Strand
Cover Designer: Shelly Garrison
Text Designer: Regina Girard
Photographer: Brent Kane

Patchwork Showcase: Simple Quilts with Big Impact
©2004 by Nancy Mahoney

That Patchwork Place® is an imprint
of Martingale & Company®.

Martingale & Company
20205 144th Avenue NE
Woodinville, WA 98072-8478 USA
www.martingale-pub.com

Printed in China
09 08 07 06 05 04   8 7 6 5 4 3 2 1

Mission Statement

Dedicated to providing quality products
and service to inspire creativity.

Library of Congress Cataloging-in-Publication Data
Mahoney, Nancy.
    Patchwork showcase : simple quilts with big impact / Nancy Mahoney.
        p. cm.
    "That Patchwork Place"
    ISBN 1-56477-554-2
    1. Patchwork—Patterns. 2. Quilting. 3. Patchwork quilts. I. Title.
    TT835 .M2715497 2004
    746 .46—dc22
                                            2004003596

CONTENTS

INTRODUCTION

This book was created with today's busy quilter in mind. While the patterns started as traditional blocks, the quilt projects offer a twist on color and a variety of clever cutting and piecing techniques to make the stitching a breeze.

If you are looking for triangle-free projects, you'll love "Spring Bouquet" on page 47 and "Indigo Chain" on page 61. You simply rotary cut strips, squares, and rectangles to make these quick and easy quilts.

If you've made a few quilts and are looking for more challenging projects, you'll want to try "Tobacco Rose" on page 22 and "Bird of Paradise" on page 84. These intricate-looking designs are not hard to make using easy shortcut techniques.

Projects such as "Romancing the Blues" on page 57 and "Funny Farm" on page 69 have large center squares perfect for the many novelty and conversation prints available today. "Whirligig" on page 50 and "Star Babies" on page 65 are wonderful, easy children's quilts. You'll find small quilts such as the adorable "Memory Garden" on page 77, which is extra quick and easy to make, and large quilts like the stunning "Stars of Provence" on page 92, which is made with only nine blocks.

In short, there's something for everyone in this project-packed collection, from small and sweet to big and bold. I know you'll enjoy making these easy, eye-catching quilts. The only dilemma will be which one to make first!

QUILTMAKING BASICS

On the following pages, you will find valuable information for the successful completion of your quilt. The timesaving techniques are ideal for both beginners and experienced quiltmakers.

Fabric Selection

Select good-quality, 100%-cotton fabrics. They hold their shape well and are easy to handle. Yardage requirements are provided for all of the projects and are based on 40" of usable fabric after preshrinking.

All of the quilts in this book began with the fabric selection. I often start by choosing a multicolored print to use as the main fabric. Next, I select a background fabric. Then I decide which pieces in the design will be background fabric and which will be the main fabric. Finally, for the remaining pieces in the quilt, I use the main fabric to select additional fabrics to complete the palette and complement the design. Remember: The background fabric does not need to be a light value. I often use yellow or gold—or a dark color such as black—as a background fabric, the same as I would a beige- or cream-colored fabric.

Theme, novelty, or conversation prints are printed fabrics based on a theme, scene, or other large-scale motif. Select one fun print that you really want to use, and then choose the rest of the fabrics based on the colors in that print.

When selecting fabrics, include prints that vary in design, scale, and texture. Many fabric manufacturers design fabric collections that not only are coordinated, but also offer prints with a variety of scale and texture within the same group. By using fabrics from one collection as a starting point, you can select the rest of the fabrics for your quilt more easily.

With the variety of fabrics available today, quilts are no longer limited to the tried-and-true plan of one light, one medium, and one dark fabric. We all see color differently and have our favorite color combinations. Choose prints and colors that *you* like, and you will almost certainly be pleased with the results.

Rotary Cutting

Note: *Rotary-cutting instructions are written for the right-handed quilter; reverse if you are left-handed.*

Instructions for rotary cutting are provided whenever possible. If you are unfamiliar with rotary cutting, refer to *Shortcuts: A Concise Guide to Rotary Cutting* by Donna Lynn Thomas (That Patchwork Place, 1999) for more detailed rotary-cutting instructions. All measurements include ¼"-wide seam allowances.

Your rotary-cutter blade is extremely sharp, and you can cut yourself before you realize it. Always keep the blade guard in place until you are ready to make a cut and close the blade immediately after cutting. When not in use, keep your rotary cutter in a safe place, away from children and pets.

Cutting Strips

It is essential that you cut strips at an exact right angle to the folded edge of your fabric. Rotary cutting squares, rectangles, and other shapes begins with cutting accurate strips.

Press the fabric, and then fold it in half with the selvages together. Place the fabric on your cutting mat with the folded edge nearest to your body. Align

a Bias Square® with the fold of the fabric and place a 6" x 24" ruler to the left so that the raw edges of the fabric are covered.

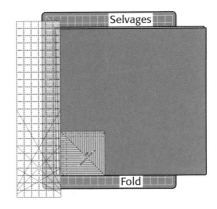

Remove the Bias Square and rotary cut along the right edge of the long ruler. Remove the ruler and gently remove the waste strip. This is called a cleanup cut.

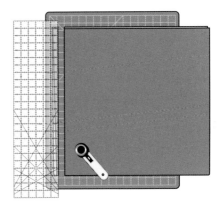

Fold the fabric again so that you are cutting four layers. Align the desired strip width on the ruler with the cut edge of the fabric, and carefully cut a strip. After cutting three or four strips, realign the Bias Square along the fold and make a new cleanup cut if necessary.

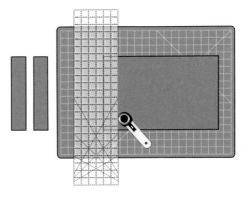

Cutting Squares and Rectangles

To cut squares and rectangles, cut strips in the desired widths and carefully cut away the selvage ends. Align the desired measurements on the ruler or Bias Square with the left edge of the strip and cut the square or rectangle. Continue cutting until you have the required number of pieces.

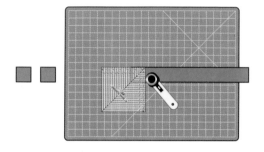

"Fussy Cutting" Special Motifs

Several quilts in this book were planned specifically to showcase a theme, novelty, or conversation print. Blocks with large open areas are perfect for showing a little printed scene or motif. If the motifs are close together, you can cut strips across the fabric width and crosscut the strips into squares, as I did in "Memory Garden" on page 77 and "Construction Zone" on page 80. However, if the motifs are widely spaced, you may want to selectively cut, or "fussy cut," the motifs. Keep in mind that fussy cutting requires more fabric and results in more fabric waste, but the results are well worth it. I fussy cut novelty prints to make the large squares in both "Funny Farm" on page 69 and "Star Babies" on page 65.

A 6" or 12" square ruler is useful for fussy cutting. Place masking tape on the ruler along the appropriate mark.

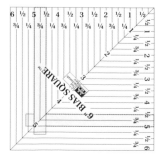

Move the marked ruler around the fabric until you find the motif you want to isolate. Cut the first two sides. Rotate the ruler and align the desired markings with the just-cut edges. Cut the remaining sides. To make best use of your fabric, you may want to plan all of your cuts first by using a pencil or blue water-soluble pen to draw the cutting lines.

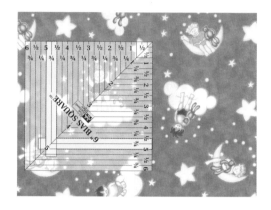

Machine Piecing

The most important aspect of machine piecing is sewing an accurate ¼" seam allowance. This enables the seams to match and the blocks to fit together properly. Some machines have a special presser foot that measures exactly ¼" from the center needle position to the edge of the foot. You can align the edge of the fabric with the edge of the presser foot, resulting in a perfect ¼" seam allowance. Some machines allow you to move the needle position to the right or left so the resulting seam is ¼" from the fabric edge to the stitching line.

If your machine doesn't have either of these features, you can create your own seam guide. Place an accurate ruler or a piece of graph paper under the presser foot and lower the needle onto the ¼" marking. Mark the seam allowance by placing a piece of masking tape at the edge of the ruler or paper. Be careful not to cover the feed dogs on your sewing machine. Use several layers of masking tape, building a raised edge to guide your fabric. You can also use moleskin or a magnetic seam guide.

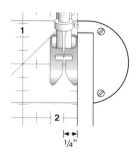

To test the accuracy of your ¼"-wide seam:

1. Cut two rectangles of fabric, each 1¼" x 3".
2. Sew the rectangles together, using the edge of the presser foot or your seam guide; press. The sewn strip should measure exactly 2" wide. If not, adjust the needle or seam guide and try again.

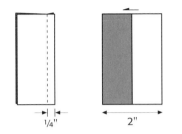

Positioning Pins

A positioning pin helps you match two points. Insert a positioning pin through the back of the first triangle, right at the triangle's tip. Separate the two triangle pairs far enough to see the tip of the second triangle and push the pin straight through that tip to establish the matching point. (Do not lock the positioning pin; let it remain loose.) Place and lock a pin on either side of the positioning pin, and then pin the remainder of the seam normally. Remove the positioning pin before stitching.

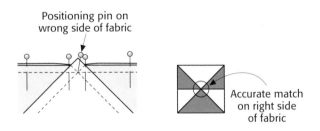

Positioning pin on wrong side of fabric

Accurate match on right side of fabric

The X Mark

When triangles are joined to other fabric pieces, the stitching lines cross on the back, creating an X at the seam line. Stitch through the center of the X to maintain a crisp point on your triangles.

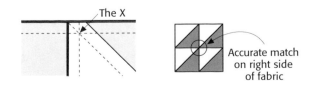

The X

Accurate match on right side of fabric

Opposing Seams

When stitching one unit to another, press seams that must match in opposite directions. The opposing seams hold each other in place and evenly distribute the fabric bulk. Whenever possible, plan pressing to take advantage of opposing seams. This is especially important in strip piecing.

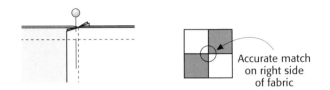

Accurate match on right side of fabric

Easing

When you must sew two pieces together, and one piece is slightly longer than the other, you need to ease the pieces together. With the shorter piece on top, pin the points that must match, the ends, and areas in between as necessary, distributing the excess fabric. Stitch the seam. The feed dogs, combined with a gentle tug, will ease the fullness of the longer piece.

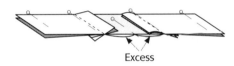

Excess

Pressing

Carefully press your work after stitching each seam. Pressing arrows are included in the project illustrations when it is necessary to press the seams in a specific direction. When no arrows are indicated, you can press the seams in either direction. Unless otherwise indicated, press seams toward the darker fabric or toward the section with fewer seams.

Helpful Tip

When joining four fabric pieces or units, try this technique to create opposing seams and reduce bulk where the seams come together. After the seam is sewn, remove one or two stitches from the seam allowance with your seam ripper as shown. Gently reposition the seam allowances to evenly distribute the fabric. Press the seams in opposite directions.

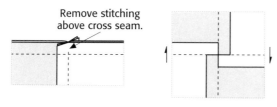

Remove stitching above cross seam.

Back of Four-Patch Unit

Half-Square and Quarter-Square Triangles

Many quilts in this book are made with half-square and quarter-square triangles. An important difference between the two is the triangles' position relative to the grain (the direction the threads run) and the bias (a line diagonal to the grain). On a half-square triangle, the short sides of the triangle are cut on grain, and the long side is cut on the bias. On a quarter-square triangle, the long side is cut on grain, and the short sides are cut on the bias. It is important to recognize the difference, because an edge that is cut on grain provides stability. An edge that is cut on the bias is quite stretchy.

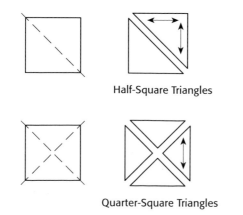

Half-Square Triangles

Quarter-Square Triangles

Half-Square-Triangle Units

When two half-square triangles are sewn together to make a square, the result is commonly called a half-square-triangle unit. The method described here is one of the easiest, fastest, and most accurate ways to make half-square-triangle units. I use this method when I need to make many smaller (less than 3") matching half-square-triangle units. Long bias strips are sewn together to make a strip set. Segments are cut from this strip set, and the segments are cut into squares.

1. Layer both fabrics with the right sides facing up.

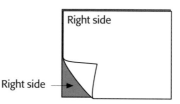

Right side

Right side

2. Beginning at one corner, place a long ruler at a 45° angle to the bottom edge of the fabric. Cut along the edge of the ruler. Using the first cut as a guide, cut bias strips in the required width for the quilt you are making. Continue to cut the strips across the entire fabric. Be sure to keep the strips in the order in which they were cut.

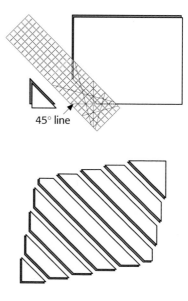

45° line

3. Separate and rearrange the strips, alternating the colors. You will have two sets of strips.

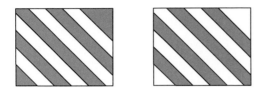

4. Sew the strips together along the bias edge, off-setting the point at the top edge ¼" as shown. Carefully press all seams toward the dark fabric. For the best result, press after sewing each seam.

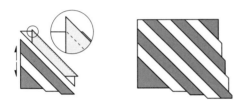

5. Position a Bias Square ruler with the 45° angle on a seam line. Align the long cutting ruler with the edge of the Bias Square so that the ends of the strip set are covered. Remove the Bias Square and make a cleanup cut along the edge of the strip set.

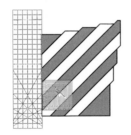

Place the 45° line of a Bias Square along a seam to accurately position the trimming ruler.

6. Cut a segment from the strip set the required width for the quilt you are making. Continue cutting segments, realigning the 45° diagonal line as needed. Maintaining a true 45° angle is critical to producing accurate units.

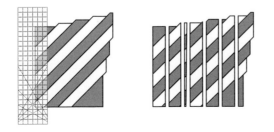

7. Working with one cut segment at a time, place a Bias Square ruler so that the edge of the ruler is even with the bottom edge of the fabric, and the 45° diagonal line is along a seam line. Cut on the right edge of the ruler. Continue cutting the segments, positioning the diagonal line of the ruler on each seam line.

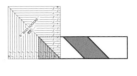

8. Turn the cut segments (or the cutting mat) around so the right-hand cuts are now at the opposite end. Working with one segment at a time, position the Bias Square ruler so that the edge of the ruler is even with the bottom edge of the fabric, and the 45° diagonal line is along the seam line. Cut on the right edge of the ruler to complete one half-square-triangle unit. Repeat with all segments.

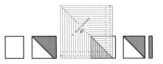

Helpful Tip

If you have fabric left over from the strip-set segments, cut smaller half-square-triangle units to use in another project. They accumulate in no time, ready for making a scrappy quilt.

Making Strip Sets

You can make multiple units more accurately and efficiently if you sew strips into strip sets and then crosscut them into segments. By using a rotary cutter, you can cut many pieces at the same time and eliminate the use of templates. The following steps describe how to make strip sets for a four-patch unit, but you can use the same process for constructing other strip sets and units.

1. Cut the number of strips in the required width for the quilt you are making. Arrange the strips in the correct color combinations. With right side together, sew the two strips together along the long edges. Press the seams toward the dark fabric.

2. Place one strip set on top of the other, right sides together, with the light fabric on top of the dark fabric.

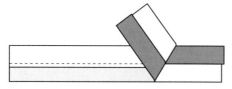

3. Trim the ends of the strip sets and cut the strip sets into segments of the desired width.

4. Stitch the segment pairs together using a ¼"-wide seam allowance.

Four-Patch Unit

Making Flying-Geese Units

Several quilts in this book contain flying-geese units. Here is a quick and accurate method for making these units using only squares and rectangles.

1. On the wrong side of two squares, draw a diagonal line from corner to corner with a ruler and the marking tool of your choice.

Wrong side of fabric

2. Place a marked square on one end of a rectangle, right sides together and raw edges aligned. Stitch directly on the marked line. Trim away the excess fabric, leaving a ¼" seam allowance. Press the seam toward the square.

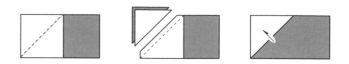

3. Place the second marked square on the other end of the rectangle, right sides together and raw edges aligned. Stitch directly on the marked line. Trim away the excess fabric, leaving a ¼" seam allowance. Press the seam toward the square.

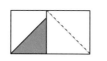

Flying-Geese Unit

Borders with Overlapped Corners

The simplest border to make is a border with overlapped corners. Most of the quilts in this book have this type of border. You will save fabric if you attach the border to the longer sides of the quilt top first, and then stitch the border to the remaining two sides. Unless noted otherwise, yardage requirements for narrow borders (less than 2" wide) are based on cutting strips across the width of the fabric and joining them end to end as needed to achieve the required length.

Joining Crosswise Strips with a Diagonal Seam

To join cross-grained strips (cut across the width of the fabric) with a diagonal seam, sew the ends of the strips at right angles, with right sides together. Stitch across the diagonal as shown on page 11 and trim ¼" from the seam line. Join all the strips end to end to make one long continuous strip, and press the seams open. Then measure the quilt top (as described below), cut the borders from the long strip, and attach as directed.

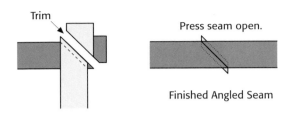

Trim

Press seam open.

Finished Angled Seam

Measuring for Length of Border Strips

To find the correct measurement for the border strips, always measure through the center of the quilt, not at the outside edges. This ensures that the borders are of equal length on opposite sides of the quilt and brings the outer edges in line with the center dimension. Otherwise, your quilt may not be square.

1. Measure the length of the quilt top from top to bottom through the center. Cut two border strips to this measurement, piecing as necessary.

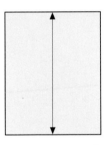

Measure center of
quilt, top to bottom.

2. Mark the center of each border strip and the quilt top. Pin the borders to the sides of the quilt top, matching centers and ends. Ease or slightly stretch the quilt top to fit the border strip as necessary.

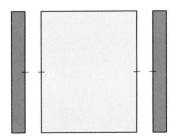

Mark centers.

3. Sew the side borders in place and press the seams toward the border strips.

4. Measure the width of the quilt top from side to side through the center (including the borders just added) to determine the length of the top and bottom border strips. Cut two border strips to this measurement, piecing as necessary. Mark the center of the border strips and the quilt top. Pin the borders to the top and bottom of the quilt top, matching centers and ends. Ease or slightly stretch the quilt top to fit the border strip as necessary.

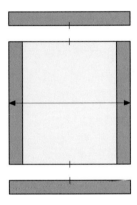

Measure center of quilt,
side to side, including
borders. Mark centers.

5. Sew the top and bottom borders in place and press the seams toward the border strips.

Borders with Corner Squares

"Forever Yours Stars" on page 26 and "Funny Farm" on page 69 are examples of quilts that include squares in the corners of their outer borders.

1. Measure the quilt top through the center to determine its width and length. Cut two border strips to each of those measurements, piecing as necessary.

2. Mark the center of the border strips and the quilt top. Pin the side borders to the sides of the quilt top, matching centers and ends. Easing as necessary, stitch the borders in place and press the seams toward the border strips.

3. Cut corner squares as indicated in the project instructions. Stitch a corner square to each end of

the top and bottom border strips; press toward the border strips. Pin the borders to the top and bottom edges of the quilt top, matching centers and ends. Easing as necessary, stitch the borders in place and press the seams toward the border strips.

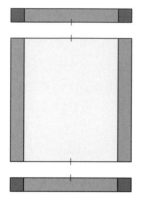

Borders with Mitered Corners

Mitered borders have a diagonal seam where the borders meet in the corners. Certain fabrics look better when used in borders with mitered corners. See "Stars of Provence" (detail below) on page 92 for a good example.

A Mitered Corner
For a full view of this quilt, see page 92.

1. Estimate the finished outside dimensions of your quilt top, including the borders. Cut border strips to this length plus at least ½" for seam allowances. To be safe, give yourself some leeway by adding 3" to 4".

2. Mark the center of the quilt-top edges and the border strips.

3. Measure the quilt top through the center to determine its width and length.

4. Place a pin at each end of the side border strips equidistant from the center to mark the length of the quilt top. Repeat with the top and bottom borders to mark the width.

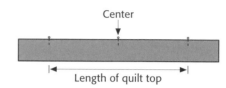

Center

Length of quilt top

5. Pin the side border strips to the quilt top, matching the centers. Line up the pins at either end of the border strip with the quilt edges and pin the border strip to the quilt. Stitch, beginning and ending with a backstitch ¼" from the raw edges of the quilt top. Repeat with the top and bottom border strips. Press seams toward the border strips.

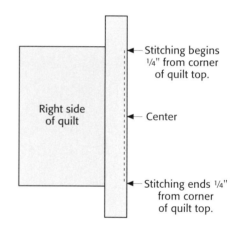

Stitching begins ¼" from corner of quilt top.

Right side of quilt

Center

Stitching ends ¼" from corner of quilt top.

6. Lay the first corner to be mitered on the ironing board. Fold under one border strip at a 45° angle to the neighboring strip. Use a square ruler to check that the outside corner is a perfect 90° angle. Press the fold and pin as shown.

7. Fold the quilt top with the right sides together, lining up the edges of the border. If necessary, use a ruler and pencil to draw a line on the pressed crease to make the line more visible. Stitch directly on the pressed crease, beginning at the seam line and sewing away from the seam toward the outside edges.

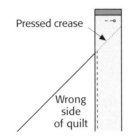

Pressed crease

Wrong side of quilt

8. Trim the excess border fabric at a 45° angle, leaving a ¼"-wide seam allowance. Press the seam open.

9. Repeat to miter the remaining corners.

Making the Backing

Most quilts consist of three layers: the quilt top, backing, and batting. To make your quilt backing, cut a piece of fabric 4" to 6" larger than the quilt top. For larger quilts, you will probably need to piece the backing from two or more widths of fabric. You can run the seam horizontally or vertically, unless the fabric is a print that is best viewed from a specific direction. Trim off the selvages before sewing the pieces together and press the seams open to reduce the bulk.

If your backing is just a bit too narrow for the quilt top, experiment with a little creative piecing. You can place the seams anywhere you want. Two possible arrangements are shown below.

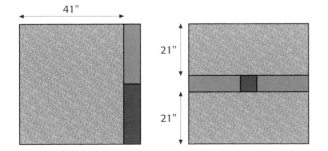

41"

21"

21"

Preparing the Batting

The type of batting you choose will depend on whether you plan to hand or machine quilt your quilt top. Generally, the thinner the batting—whether cotton or polyester—the easier it is to hand quilt. For machine quilting, you may want to use cotton batting that has a scrim, or thin mesh, that the fibers are woven through. A scrim helps stabilize the batting, so you can place quilting lines farther apart, but it can be difficult to hand quilt. You can buy batting by the yard or packaged in standard bed sizes. If you are using prepackaged batting, open the package and smooth the batting out flat. Allow it to rest in this position for at least 24 hours. Plan for at least 2" of extra batting around all edges of the quilt top.

Layering the Quilt

Follow these steps to put the three layers of your quilt together:

1. Spread a well-pressed backing, wrong side up, on a flat, clean surface. Anchor it with pins or masking tape. Be careful not to stretch the backing out of shape.

2. Center and spread the batting over the backing, smoothing out any wrinkles.

3. Center and place the pressed quilt top, right side up, on top of the batting. Smooth out any wrinkles and make sure the edges of the quilt top are parallel to the edges of the backing. Smooth from the center out and along straight lines to ensure that the blocks and borders remain straight.

   For hand quilting, baste with needle and thread, starting in the center and working diagonally to each corner. Continue basting in a grid of horizontal and vertical lines 6" to 8" apart. To finish, baste around the edges about ⅛" from the edge of the quilt top.

For machine quilting, baste the layers with #2 rustproof safety pins. Place pins 4" to 6" apart; try to avoid areas where you intend to quilt.

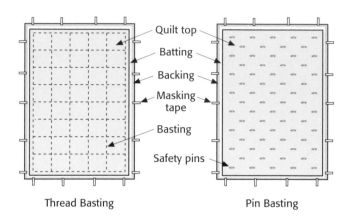

Thread Basting   Pin Basting

Quilting

When deciding on your quilting designs, consider the desired effect. As a rule, the quilting should enhance the quilt rather than distract the viewer.

The two most common forms of quilting are quilting in the ditch and outline quilting. Both can be done either by hand or machine. To decide how much quilting is needed, use the general rule that no unquilted space should exceed 4" x 4". The amount of quilting should be consistent over the entire quilt so that the quilt remains square and free from distortion. A common mistake is to heavily quilt the center of the quilt top and do very little quilting in the border.

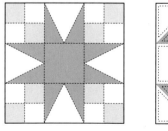

Quilting in the Ditch   Outline Quilting

Hand Quilting

To quilt by hand, you will need short, sturdy needles (called Betweens), quilting thread, and a thimble to fit the middle finger of your sewing hand. Most quilters use a frame or hoop to support their work.

Use the smallest needle you can comfortably handle; the finer the needle, the smaller your stitches will be.

1. Thread your needle with a single strand of quilting thread about 18" long. Make a small knot and insert the needle in the top layer about 1" from the point where you want to start stitching. Pull the needle out at the point where quilting will begin and gently pull the thread until the knot pops through the fabric and into the batting.

2. Place one hand underneath the quilt so you can feel the point of the needle with the tip of your first finger when a stitch is taken. Take small, evenly spaced stitches through all three layers. Rock the needle up and down until you have three or four stitches on the needle.

3. To end a line of quilting, make a small knot close to the last stitch, and then backstitch, running the thread a needle's length through the batting. Gently pull the thread until the knot pops into the batting; clip the thread at the quilt's surface.

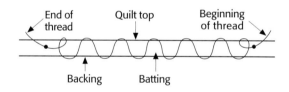

Machine Quilting

Machine quilting is suitable for all types and sizes of quilts and allows you to complete a quilt quickly.

For straight-line quilting, it is extremely helpful to have a walking foot to help feed the layers through the machine without shifting or puckering. Some machines have a built-in walking foot; other machines require a separate attachment.

Walking Foot Attachment

For free-motion quilting, you need a darning foot and the ability to drop the feed dogs on your machine. With free-motion quilting, you do not turn the fabric under the needle but instead guide the fabric in the direction of the design. Because the feed dogs are lowered, the stitch length is determined by the speed at which you run the machine and feed the fabric under the foot. Use free-motion quilting to outline a quilt pattern in the fabric or to create stippling and many other designs.

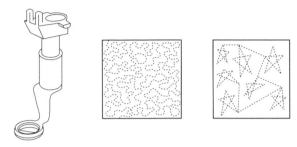

Darning Foot

Helpful Tips

❖ Plan a design that has continuous long lines. Complete all of the straight-line quilting with the walking foot, and then switch to the darning foot, lower the feed dogs, and start the free-motion quilting.

❖ Use a sewing-machine needle with a large eye, such as a 90/14, that will not shred the thread.

❖ Before you begin quilting, make a sample square consisting of two 6" squares of fabric and a 6" square of batting. Practice moving the fabric with your hands and controlling the machine's speed until you feel comfortable. Look at both sides of the sample to check the thread tension; adjust the tension if necessary.

❖ Start and stop each quilting line by shortening the stitch length for the first and last ⅛" to ¼".

❖ For more information on machine quilting, refer to Machine Quilting Made Easy! by Maurine Noble (That Patchwork Place, 1994).

Squaring Up a Quilt

When you complete the quilting, you will need to square up your quilt before sewing on the binding. Align a ruler with the seam line of the outer border and measure the width of the outer border in several places. Using the narrowest measurement, position a ruler along the seam line of the outer border and trim the excess batting and backing from all four sides. Use a large square ruler to square up each corner.

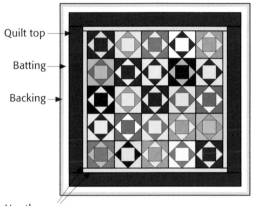

Quilt top →
Batting →
Backing →

Use these seam
lines as a guide.

Binding

The binding is a wonderful chance to add to the overall look of your quilt. If you want the binding to disappear, use the same fabric for the binding as for the outer border. If you prefer the binding to frame the outer border or act as an additional border, then use a fabric different from the outer border. You can also make the binding from leftover strips, provided the strips are the correct width or can be cut down to the desired width. "Forever Yours Stars" on page 26 has a binding made from leftover strips.

I prefer a double-fold binding made from straight-grain strips. A straight-grain binding is easier to work with and takes less fabric than a bias-cut binding. I cut 2"-wide strips for my binding. Depending on your batting choice, you may want to cut the strips wider. You will need enough strips to go around the perimeter of the quilt plus about 10" for making seams and turning corners. The number of strips is specified for each quilt. If you plan to attach a sleeve to the back of your quilt, turn to "Adding a Sleeve" on page 17 and attach it now, before you bind the edges.

1. Cut 2"-wide strips across the width of the fabric as required for your quilt.

2. Join the strips at right angles and stitch across the corner as shown. Trim the excess fabric, leaving a ¼" seam allowance, and press the seams open.

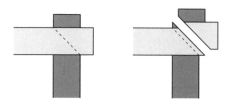

3. Fold the binding in half lengthwise, with the wrong sides together, and press.

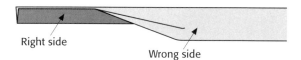

Right side

Wrong side

4. Unfold the binding at one end and turn under ¼" at a 45° angle as shown, trimming if necessary.

Fold line

5. Starting on the bottom edge of the quilt (not on a corner), stitch the binding to the quilt. Use a ¼" seam allowance. Begin stitching 3" from the start of the binding. Stop stitching ¼" from the first corner and backstitch.

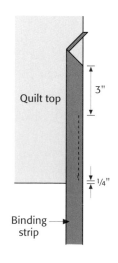

Quilt top

3"

¼"

Binding strip

6. Remove the quilt from the sewing machine. Fold the binding away from the quilt, and then fold again and pin as shown to create an angled pleat at the corner.

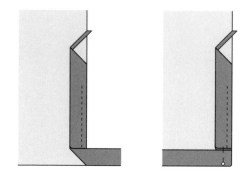

7. Start stitching at the fold of the binding. Backstitch at the beginning of the seam and then continue stitching along the edge of the quilt top. Stop ¼" from the next corner and backstitch. Repeat step 6 to form the mitered corner. Continue stitching around the quilt, repeating the mitering process at each corner.

8. When you reach the beginning of the binding, stop 3" before the starting end and backstitch. Remove the quilt from the machine. Trim the binding tail 1" longer than needed and tuck the end inside the beginning of the strip. Pin in place, making sure the strip lies flat. Stitch the rest of the binding.

9. Turn the binding to the back of the quilt. Hand stitch the binding in place with the folded edge covering the row of machine stitching. Use thread that matches the binding. At each corner, fold the binding to form a miter on the back of the quilt.

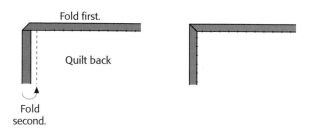

Fold first.

Quilt back

Fold second.

Adding a Sleeve

If you plan to hang your quilt, attach a sleeve or rod pocket to the back before attaching the binding.

1. From the leftover fabric, cut an 8"-wide strip of fabric equal to the width of your quilt. You may need to piece two or three strips together for larger quilts.

2. On each end of the strip, fold over ½" and then fold ½" again. Press and stitch by machine.

½" ½"

3. Fold the strip in half lengthwise, wrong sides together; baste the raw edges to the top edge of the back of your quilt. These will be secured when you sew on the binding. Your quilt should be about 1" wider than the sleeve on both sides.

Raw edges

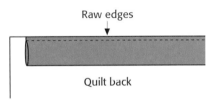

Quilt back

4. Make a little pleat in the sleeve to accommodate the thickness of the rod, and then slipstitch the ends and bottom edge of the sleeve to the backing fabric. This keeps the rod from being inserted next to the quilt backing.

Binding

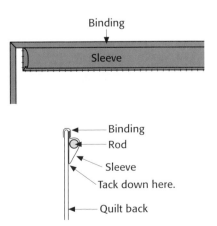

Sleeve

Binding
Rod
Sleeve
Tack down here.
Quilt back

Adding a Label

Future generations will want to know who made your quilt. A label provides important information including the name of the quilt, who made it, when, and where. You may also want to include the name of the recipient, if it is a gift, and any other interesting or important information about the quilt.

A label can be as elaborate or as simple as you desire. To make a label, use a permanent-ink pen to write all of the information on a piece of muslin or light-colored fabric. Press a piece of freezer paper to the back of the muslin to stabilize it while you write. To keep your writing straight, draw lines on the freezer paper with a fat-tipped marker as a guide. You should be able to see the lines through the fabric.

When the label is complete, remove the freezer paper and press the raw edges to the wrong side of the label. Stitch the label to the lower-right corner of the back of the quilt with a blind hem stitch.

Label from "Star Babies"
For a full front view of this quilt, see page 65.

PEAR LILY

By Nancy Mahoney
From the collection of Clothworks, featuring their Tuscan Harvest fabrics.

Finished Quilt Size: 55" x 55"

Finished Block Size: 10"

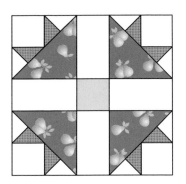

"*Pear Lily*" *is a shining example of a wonderful traditional quilt in a diagonal set. The nine Carolina Lily blocks are quick and easy to piece, and the unpieced squares are perfect for showcasing a stunning quilting design.*

Materials

Yardage is based on 42"-wide fabric.

1¾ yards of pear print for blocks and outer border

1½ yards of light background print for blocks and setting squares

⅞ yard of purple fern print for setting triangles

¾ yard of purple check for blocks and binding

⅜ yard of yellow print for blocks and inner border

3½ yards of fabric for backing

59" x 59" piece of batting

Cutting

All measurements include ¼" seam allowances. Unless otherwise noted, cut all strips from the crosswise grain. Outer (lengthwise) borders are cut long to allow for fabric shrinkage.

From the light background print, cut:
- 2 strips, 3¼" x 42"; crosscut into 18 squares, 3¼" x 3¼"
- 3 strips, 2½" x 42"; crosscut into 36 squares, 2½" x 2½"
- 5 strips, 2½" x 42"; crosscut into 36 rectangles, 2½" x 4½"
- 4 squares, 10½" x 10½"

From the purple check, cut:
- 2 strips, 3¼" x 42"; crosscut into 18 squares, 3¼" x 3¼"
- 6 strips, 2" x 42"

From the *lengthwise* grain of the pear print, cut:
- 4 strips, 5½" x 63"

From the remaining pear print, cut:
- 18 squares, 4⅞" x 4⅞"; cut once diagonally to yield 36 half-square triangles

From the yellow print, cut:
- 9 squares, 2½" x 2½"
- 5 strips, 1½" x 42"

From the purple fern print, cut:
- 2 squares, 17" x 17"; cut twice diagonally to yield 8 quarter-square side setting triangles*
- 2 squares, 10" x 10"; cut once diagonally to yield 4 half-square corner setting triangles*

   * *These are cut extra large and will be trimmed later.*

Making the Blocks

1. Using a pencil and ruler, draw a diagonal line from corner to corner on the wrong side of each 3¼" background square. Place a marked background square on a purple check square, with right sides together and raw edges aligned.

Stitch ¼" on each side of the diagonal line. Cut along the drawn diagonal line to yield two half-square-triangle units; press. Make 36 units, 2⅞" x 2⅞".

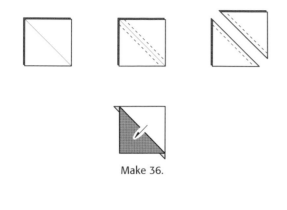

Make 36.

Helpful Tip

If the presser foot on your sewing machine measures exactly ¼" from the center of the needle to the edge of the presser foot, you can align the edge of the presser foot with the marked diagonal line to achieve a perfect ¼" seam allowance. Otherwise, after drawing a diagonal line from corner to corner, draw a line ¼" on either side of the center diagonal line. Stitch on these lines, and then cut along the first (center) line.

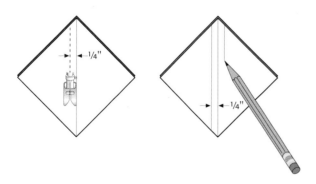

2. Cut each half-square-triangle unit once diagonally to make 72 quarter-square-triangle units.

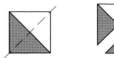

Make 72.

3. Sew two units from step 2 to a 2½" background square; press. Make 36 units.

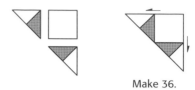

Make 36.

4. Sew a pear print triangle to a unit from step 3; press. Make 36 units.

Make 36.

5. Sew four units from step 4, a yellow square, and four background rectangles into rows as shown; press. Sew the rows together to complete the block; press. Make nine blocks.

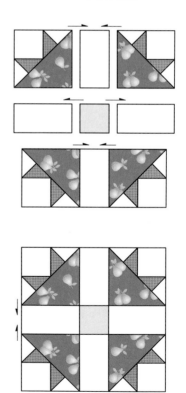

Make 9.

Assembling the Quilt Top

1. Arrange the blocks, 10½" background squares, and corner and side setting triangles in diagonal rows as shown.

2. Sew the blocks together in diagonal rows; press.

3. Sew the rows together; press.

4. Trim the outside edges and square up the corners of the quilt top, making sure to leave a ¼" seam allowance all around the outside edge. The quilt should measure 43" x 43".

Adding the Borders

Refer to "Borders with Overlapped Corners" on page 10 as needed.

1. Join the inner-border strips end to end to make a continuous strip. Measure the quilt through the center from top to bottom and cut two border strips to fit that measurement.

2. Sew the trimmed border strips to the side edges of the quilt top. Press toward the border strips.

3. Measure the quilt through the center from side to side, including the borders just added. Cut two border strips to fit that measurement.

4. Sew the trimmed border strips to the top and bottom edges of the quilt top; press.

5. Repeat steps 1–4 to measure, trim, and add the outer-border strips. (You will not need to piece the strips.) Press toward the outer-border strips.

Finishing the Quilt

For detailed instructions on the following finishing techniques, refer to pages 13–17 of "Quiltmaking Basics."

1. Cut and piece the backing fabric so it is 4" to 6" larger than the quilt top. Layer the quilt top, batting, and backing; baste.

2. Hand or machine quilt as desired. Suggestions include machine quilting in the ditch and stipple quilting in the border.

3. Square up the quilt sandwich.

4. Prepare and sew the binding to the quilt. Add a hanging sleeve, if desired, and a label.

TOBACCO ROSE

By Nancy Mahoney

From the collection of Clothworks, featuring their Tobacco Rose fabrics.

Finished Quilt Size: 48½" x 61½"

Finished Block Size: 12"

A wonderful floral fabric inspired this stunning quilt. Very light yellow and darker brown prints give the Pyramids block dimension and movement, while a variety of red and brown prints add visual interest. The use of a consistent background and light brown print in each block gives the design continuity.

Materials

Yardage is based on 42"-wide fabric.

2 yards of red large-scale floral print for blocks, border, and binding

1⅛ yards of light brown print for blocks

½ yard of light yellow print for blocks

⅜ yard of red small-scale floral print for sashing

⅜ yard *each* of 2 medium yellow prints for blocks and sashing squares

1 fat quarter *each* of 3 red prints for blocks

1 fat quarter *each* of 4 medium and dark brown prints for blocks

3¼ yards of fabric for backing

54" x 66" piece of batting

Cutting

All measurements include ¼" seam allowance. Unless otherwise noted, cut all strips from the crosswise grain. Outer (lengthwise) borders are cut long to allow for fabric shrinkage.

From the light brown print, cut:
- 13 strips, 2⅝" x 42"; crosscut into 192 squares, 2⅝" x 2⅝"

From *each* medium yellow print, cut:
- 24 rectangles, 2⅝" x 4¾" (48 total)

From *one* medium yellow print, cut:
- 6 squares, 1½" x 1½"

From *each* red fat quarter, cut:
- 3 squares, 4¾" x 4¾" (9 total)
- 12 rectangles, 2⅝" x 4¾" (36 total)

From the *lengthwise* grain of the red large-scale floral print, cut:
- 4 strips, 5½" x 72"
- 12 strips, 2" x 42"

From the remaining red large-scale floral print, cut:
- 3 squares, 4¾" x 4¾"
- 12 rectangles, 2⅝" x 4¾"

From the light yellow print, cut:
- 3 strips, 4¼" x 42"; crosscut into 24 squares, 4¼" x 4¼". Cut twice diagonally to yield 96 triangles.

From *each* medium and dark brown fat quarter, cut:
- 12 squares, 2⅝" x 2⅝" (48 total)
- 6 squares, 3⅞" x 3⅞" (24 total); cut once diagonally to yield 48 triangles

From the red small-scale floral print, cut:
- 6 strips, 1½" x 42"; crosscut into 17 strips, 1½" x 12½"

Making the Blocks

For detailed instructions, refer to "Making Flying-Geese Units" on page 10.

1. Stitch two light brown squares to a medium yellow rectangle; press. Make 48, in matching sets of 4.

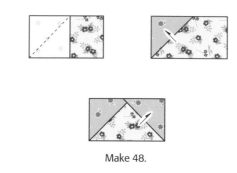

Make 48.

2. Repeat step 1, using two light brown squares and a red rectangle; press. Make 48, in matching sets of 4.

Make 48.

3. Sew two light yellow triangles to a medium or dark brown square as shown; press. Make 48, in matching sets of 4.

Make 48.

4. Sew four matching units *each* from steps 1, 2, and 3, a red square, and four matching brown triangles into diagonal rows as shown; press. Sew the rows together to complete the block; press. Make 12 blocks.

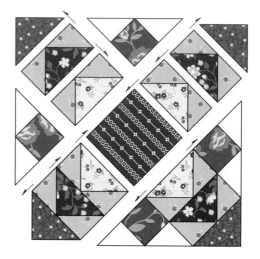

Make 12.

Assembling the Quilt Top

1. Sew three blocks and two red 1½" x 12½" strips together to make a row; press. Make four rows.

Make 4.

2. Sew three remaining red strips and two medium yellow squares together to make a row; press. Make three rows.

Make 3.

3. Sew the rows of blocks and sashing together; press.

Adding the Borders

For detailed instructions, refer to "Borders with Overlapped Corners" on page 10 as needed.

1. Measure the quilt through the center from top to bottom, and cut two red border strips to fit that measurement.

2. Sew the trimmed border strips to the side edges of the quilt top. Press toward the border strips.

3. Measure the quilt through the center from side to side, including the borders just added. Cut two border strips to fit that measurement.

4. Sew the trimmed border strips to the top and bottom edges of the quilt top; press.

Finishing the Quilt

For detailed instructions on the following finishing techniques, refer to pages 13–17 of "Quiltmaking Basics."

1. Cut and piece the backing fabric so it is 4" to 6" larger than the quilt top. Layer the quilt top, batting, and backing; baste.

2. Hand or machine quilt as desired. Suggestions include machine quilting in the ditch and quilting straight, parallel lines in the border.

3. Square up the quilt sandwich.

4. Prepare and sew the binding to the quilt. Add a hanging sleeve, if desired, and a label.

FOREVER YOURS STARS

By Nancy Mahoney

From the collection of Clothworks, featuring their Forever Yours fabrics.

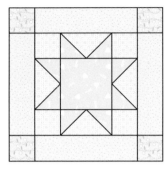

Finished Quilt Size: 48½" x 60½"

Finished Block Size: 12"

Simple squares and rectangles surround classic Sawtooth Star blocks to create this quick and easy quilt. The wonderful wash of pastel prints is a soothing choice for young and old alike.

Materials

Yardage is based on 42"-wide fabric.

1¾ yards of yellow print for blocks and outer border

1 fat quarter *each* of 5 blue prints for blocks, inner border, and binding

1 fat quarter *each* of 5 pink prints for blocks, inner border, and binding

1 fat quarter *each* of 5 green prints for blocks, inner border, and binding

1 fat quarter *each* of 4 yellow prints for blocks, inner border, and binding

3¼ yards of fabric for backing

54" x 66" piece of batting

Cutting

All measurements include ¼" seam allowance. Unless otherwise noted, cut all strips from the crosswise grain. Outer (lengthwise) borders are cut long to allow for fabric shrinkage.

From the *lengthwise* grain of the 1¾ yards of yellow print, cut:
- 4 strips, 4½" x 63"

From the remaining 1¾ yards of yellow print, cut:
- 16 squares, 2½" x 2½"
- 4 rectangles, 2½" x 4½"
- 1 square, 4½" x 4½"
- 4 rectangles, 2½" x 8½"

From *each* of 2 yellow print fat quarters, cut:
- 8 squares, 2½" x 2½" (16 total)
- 4 rectangles, 2½" x 4½" (8 total)
- 4 rectangles, 2½" x 8½" (8 total)
- 1 strip, 2" x 21" (2 total)

From *each* remaining yellow print fat quarter, cut:
- 11 squares, 2½" x 2½" (22 total)
- 1 square, 4½" x 4½" (2 total)
- 1 rectangle, 2½" x 8½" (2 total)

From *each* of 3 green print fat quarters, cut:
- 12 squares, 2½" x 2½" (36 total)
- 1 square, 4½" x 4½" (3 total)
- 4 rectangles, 2½" x 8½" (12 total)

From *each* remaining green print fat quarter, cut:
- 8 squares, 2½" x 2½" (16 total)
- 4 rectangles, 2½" x 4½" (8 total)
- 2 strips, 2" x 21" (4 total)
- 3 rectangles, 2½" x 8½" (6 total; 1 is extra)

From *each* of 3 pink print fat quarters, cut:
- 12 squares, 2½" x 2½" (36 total)
- 1 square, 4½" x 4½" (3 total)
- 4 rectangles, 2½" x 8½" (12 total)
- 1 strip, 2" x 21" (3 total)

From *each* remaining pink print fat quarter, cut:
- 13 squares, 2½" x 2½" (26 total)
- 8 rectangles, 2½" x 4½" (16 total)
- 1 square, 4½" x 4½" (2 total)
- 2 pink rectangles, 2½" x 8½" (4 total; 1 is extra)

From *each* of 3 blue print fat quarters, cut:

- 12 squares, 2½" x 2½" (36 total)
- 4 rectangles, 2½" x 4½" (12 total)
- 1 strip, 2" x 21" (3 total)
- 2 squares, 4½" x 4½" (6 total; 1 is extra)

From *each* remaining blue print fat quarter, cut:

- 10 squares, 2½" x 2½" (20 total)
- 8 rectangles, 2½" x 8½" (16 total)

Making the Blocks

Note: You may find it helpful to presort one 4½" square and eight 2½" squares in one matching color/print; and four 2½" squares and four 2½" x 4½" rectangles in a different matching color/print for each star unit.

For detailed instructions, refer to "Making Flying-Geese Units" on page 10.

1. Stitch two matching 2½" squares to a 2½" x 4½" rectangle; press. Make 48, in matching sets of 4.

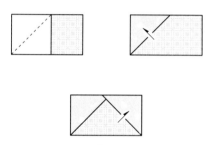

Make 48.

2. Sew four matching units from step 1, a 4½" square from the same print as the small triangles, and four 2½" squares from the same print as the large triangles into rows as shown; press. Sew the rows together; press. Make 12 star units.

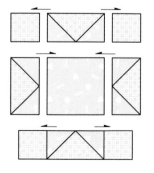

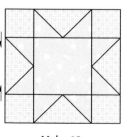

Make 12.

3. Sew four matching 2½" x 8½" rectangles, four matching 2½" squares, and a star unit from step 2 into rows as shown; press. Sew the rows together to complete the block; press. Make 12 blocks.

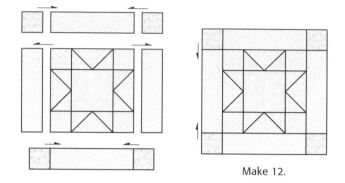

Make 12.

Assembling the Quilt Top

1. Arrange and sew the blocks in four rows of three blocks each; press.

2. Sew the rows together; press.

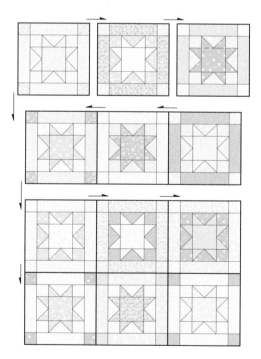

Adding the Borders

For detailed instructions, refer to "Borders with Corner Squares" on page 11.

1. Sew four assorted 2½" x 8½" rectangles and eight assorted 2½" squares together to make a side inner-border strip; press. Make two.

Make 2.

2. Sew three assorted 2½" x 8½" rectangles and eight assorted 2½" squares together to make the top inner-border strip; press. Repeat for the bottom inner-border strip.

Make 2.

3. Sew the side inner-border strips to the side edges of the quilt top; press. Sew the top and bottom inner-border strips to the top and bottom edges; press.

4. Measure the quilt through the center from top to bottom and cut two side outer-border strips to fit that measurement. Measure the quilt through the center from side to side and cut a top and a bottom outer-border strip to fit that measurement.

5. Sew the side outer-border strips to the side edges of the quilt top. Press toward the outer-border strips.

6. Sew a 4½" square to each end of the top and bottom outer-border strips; press.

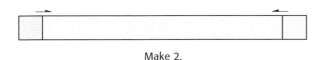

Make 2.

7. Sew the outer-border strips to the top and bottom edges of the quilt top; press.

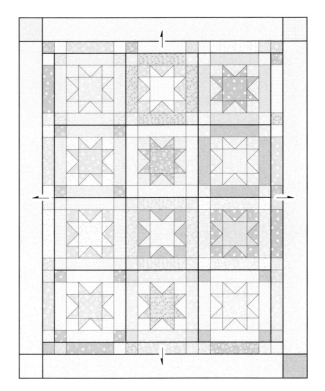

Finishing the Quilt

For detailed instructions on the following finishing techniques, refer to pages 13–17 of "Quiltmaking Basics."

1. Cut and piece the backing fabric so it is 4" to 6" larger than the quilt top. Layer the quilt top, batting, and backing; baste.

2. Hand or machine quilt as desired. Suggestions include machine quilting in the ditch, quilting large overlapping diamonds across the blocks, and stipple quilting in the border.

3. Square up the quilt sandwich.

4. Prepare and sew the binding to the quilt. Add a hanging sleeve, if desired, and a label.

TUSCAN STARS

By Nancy Mahoney
From the collection of Clothworks, featuring their Tuscan Harvest fabrics.

Finished Quilt Size: 55½" x 55½"

Finished Block Size: 8"

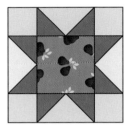

This beautiful pattern looks complex, but it's not! Sawtooth Star blocks combine with pieced sashing to create the multifaceted design so admired in any quilt. The quilt is easy to piece using only squares and rectangles— no fussy triangles. Using several prints in the same color makes the design sparkle.

Materials

Yardage is based on 42"-wide fabric.

1¾ yards of green print A for blocks, outer border, and binding

¾ yard of yellow print for Star blocks and inner border

¾ yard *each* of 2 tan prints for blocks

⅝ yard of purple print for sashing

⅜ yard of green print B for blocks

⅜ yard of green-background pear print for blocks

⅜ yard of red-background pear print for sashing

1 fat quarter *each* of 4 light floral prints for sashing

1 fat quarter *each* of 3 red prints for sashing

1 fat quarter of yellow print for sashing

3¾ yards of fabric for backing

60" x 60" piece of batting

Cutting

All measurements include ¼" seam allowances. Unless otherwise noted, cut all strips from the crosswise grain. Outer (lengthwise) borders are cut long to allow for fabric shrinkage.

From the *lengthwise* grain of green print A, cut:
- 4 strips, 5" x 63"
- 4 strips, 2" x 63"

From the remaining green print A, cut:
- 64 squares, 2½" x 2½"

From green print B, cut:
- 4 strips, 2½" x 42"; crosscut into 64 squares, 2½" x 2½"

From *each* tan print, cut:
- 8 strips, 2½" x 42"; crosscut into 56 rectangles, 2½" x 4½" (112 total)

From the ¾ yard of yellow print, cut:
- 5 strips, 2½" x 42"; crosscut into 64 squares, 2½" x 2½"
- 5 strips, 1½" x 42"

From the green-background pear print, cut:
- 16 squares, 4½" x 4½"

From the purple print, cut:
- 6 strips, 2½" x 42"; crosscut into 96 squares, 2½" x 2½"

From *each* light floral print fat quarter, cut:
- 6 squares, 4½" x 4½" (24 total)

From *each* red print fat quarter, cut:
- 24 squares, 2½" x 2½" (72 total)

From the yellow print fat quarter, cut:
- 24 squares, 2½" x 2½"

From the red-background pear print, cut:
- 9 squares, 4½" x 4½"

Making the Star Blocks

For detailed instructions, refer to "Making Flying-Geese Units" on page 10.

1. Stitch two matching (A or B) green 2½" squares to a tan rectangle; press. Make 64, in matching sets of 4.

Make 64.

2. Sew four matching units from step 1, a green-background pear square, and four yellow 2½" squares into rows as shown; press. Sew the rows together to complete the block; press. Make 16 blocks.

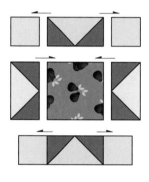 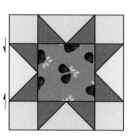

Make 16.

Making the Sashing Units

1. Use a pencil and ruler to draw a diagonal line from corner to corner on the wrong side of each purple square. Place two marked squares on opposite corners of a floral print square, right sides together and raw edges aligned. Stitch directly on the pencil line. Trim away the excess fabric, leaving a ¼" seam allowance; press.

2. Repeat step 1, stitching a marked purple square to each remaining corner of the floral print square; press. Make 24.

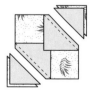

Make 24.

3. Stitch two matching red 2½" squares to a tan rectangle; press. Make 36.

Make 36.

4. Stitch two yellow 2½" squares to a tan rectangle; press. Make 12.

Make 12.

5. Sew two units from step 3 to a unit from step 2; press. Make 12 and label them sashing unit A.

Sashing Unit A
Make 12.

6. Sew a unit from step 3 and a unit from step 4 to a unit from step 2; press. Make 12 and label them sashing unit B.

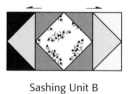

Sashing Unit B
Make 12.

Assembling the Quilt Top

1. Sew four Star blocks and three A sashing units together to make a row as shown; press. Make two rows and label them row A.

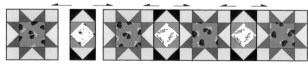

Row A
Make 2.

2. Sew four Star blocks and three B sashing units together to make a row as shown; press. Make two rows and label them row B.

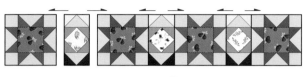

Row B
Make 2.

3. Sew two A sashing units, two B sashing units, and three red-background 4½" squares together to make a row as shown; press. Make three rows and label them row C.

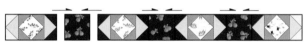

Row C
Make 3.

4. Arrange and sew the A, B, and C rows together as shown; press.

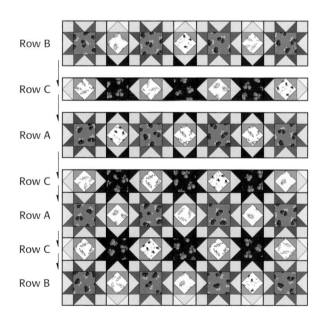

Row B
Row C
Row A
Row C
Row A
Row C
Row B

Adding the Borders

For detailed instructions, refer to "Borders with Overlapped Corners" on page 10.

1. Join the inner-border strips end to end to make a continuous strip. Measure the quilt through the center from top to bottom and cut two border strips to fit that measurement.

2. Sew the trimmed border strips to the side edges of the quilt top. Press toward the border strips.

3. Measure the quilt through the center from side to side, including the borders just added. Cut two border strips to fit that measurement.

4. Sew the trimmed border strips to the top and bottom edges of the quilt top; press.

5. Repeat steps 1–4 to measure, trim, and add the outer-border strips. (You will not need to piece the strips.) Press toward the outer-border strips.

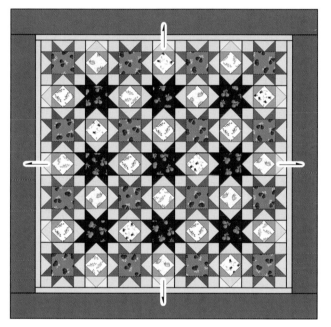

Finishing the Quilt

For detailed instructions on the following finishing techniques, refer to pages 13–17 of "Quiltmaking Basics."

1. Cut and piece the backing fabric so it is 4" to 6" larger than the quilt top. Layer the quilt top, batting, and backing; baste.

2. Hand or machine quilt as desired. Suggestions include machine quilting in the ditch, quilting diamonds in the center squares, and quilting swirls and leaves in the borders.

3. Square up the quilt sandwich.

4. Prepare and sew the binding to the quilt. Add a hanging sleeve, if desired, and a label.

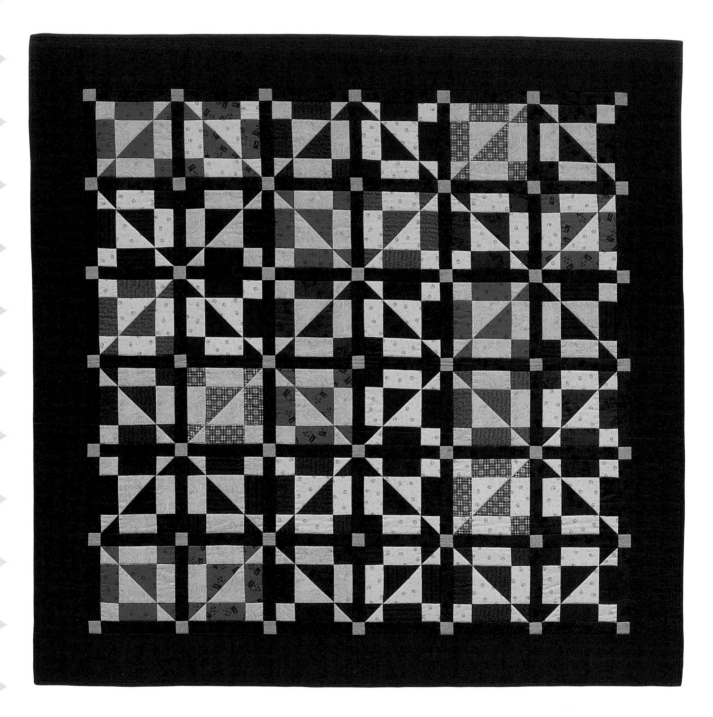

By Nancy Mahoney

From the collection of Clothworks, featuring their Glory Garden fabrics.

Finished Quilt Size: 51½" x 51½"

Finished Block Size: 6"

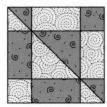

You'll be amazed at how quickly and easily this quilt goes together! Simple, two-fabric blocks combine with narrow sashing to create the illusion of waves. While a dominance of red and blue prints gives this quilt a patriotic touch, you'll want to use it all year long.

Materials

Yardage is based on 42"-wide fabric.

1⅝ yards of red print for blocks, border, and binding

1 yard of navy print for blocks and sashing

⅞ yard *each* of 2 background prints for blocks

1 fat quarter *each* of 2 green prints for blocks

1 fat quarter *each* of 2 purple prints for blocks

1 fat quarter *each* of 2 brown prints for blocks

1 fat quarter of red print for blocks

1 fat quarter of navy print for blocks

1 fat eighth (9" x 21") of gold fabric for sashing squares

3½ yards of fabric for backing

56" x 56" piece of batting

Cutting

All measurements include ¼" seam allowance. Unless otherwise noted, cut all strips from the crosswise grain. Outer (lengthwise) borders are cut long to allow for fabric shrinkage.

From *each* background print, cut:
- 5 squares, 8" x 8" (10 total)
- 1 strip, 3⅞" x 42"; crosscut into 10 squares, 3⅞" x 3⅞" (20 total)
- 1 strip, 2" x 42"; crosscut into 18 squares, 2" x 2" (36 total)
- 4 strips, 2" x 42"; crosscut into 36 rectangles, 2" x 3½" (72 total)

From the *lengthwise* grain of the 1⅝ yards of red print, cut:
- 4 strips, 4½" x 58"
- 4 strips, 2" x 58"

From the remaining 1⅝ yards of red print, cut:
- 1 square, 8" x 8"
- 2 squares, 3⅞" x 3⅞"
- 4 squares, 2" x 2"
- 8 rectangles, 2" x 3½"

From the yard of navy print, cut:
- 15 strips, 1½" x 42"; crosscut into 84 strips, 1½" x 6½"
- 1 square, 8" x 8"
- 2 squares, 3⅞" x 3⅞"
- 3 squares, 2" x 2"
- 6 rectangles, 2" x 3½"

From the red and navy fat quarters, and one *each* of the purple, green, and brown fat quarters, cut:
- 1 square, 8" x 8" (5 total)
- 2 squares, 3⅞" x 3⅞" (10 total)
- 4 squares, 2" x 2" (20 total)
- 8 rectangles, 2" x 3½" (40 total)

From *each* remaining purple, green, and brown fat quarter, cut:
- 1 square, 8" x 8" (3 total)
- 2 squares, 3⅞" x 3⅞" (6 total)
- 3 squares, 2" x 2" (9 total)
- 6 rectangles, 2" x 3½" (18 total)

From the gold fat eighth, cut:
- 4 strips, 1½" x 21"; crosscut into 49 squares, 1½" x 1½"

Making the Blocks

For detailed instructions, refer to "Half-Square-Triangle Units" on page 8.

1. Pair each 8" background square with an 8" red, navy, purple, green, or brown square, right sides facing up. Cut and piece 2½"-wide bias strips to make 18 strip sets. Cut the strip sets to make 72 half-square-triangle units in matching sets of 2, each 2" x 2".

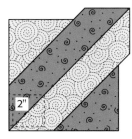

Make 18 strip sets.
Cut 72 units.

2. Using a pencil and ruler, draw a diagonal line from corner to corner on the wrong side of each 3⅞" background square. Place a marked background square on a red, navy, purple, green, or brown 3⅞" square (in a combination that matches a unit from step 1), with right sides together and raw edges aligned. Stitch ¼" on each side of the diagonal line. Cut along the drawn diagonal line to yield two half-square-triangle units; press. Make 36 units, 3½" x 3½".

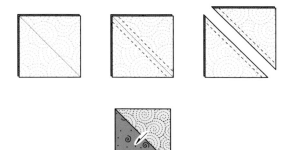

Make 36.

3. Sew a unit from step 2; two matching units from step 1; two matching background rectangles; a matching 2" background square; two matching red, navy, purple, green, or brown rectangles; and a matching 2" square into rows as shown; press. Sew the rows together to complete the block; press. Make 36 blocks.

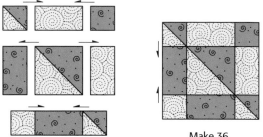

Make 36.

Assembling the Quilt Top

1. Arrange six blocks and seven 1½" x 6½" navy strips to make a row, rotating the blocks as shown. Sew the blocks and strips together; press. Make six rows.

Make 6.

2. Sew six navy strips and seven gold 1½" squares together to make a row; press. Make seven rows.

Make 7.

3. Sew the rows of blocks and sashing together, rotating the rows of blocks as shown; press.

4. Sew the trimmed border strips to the top and bottom edges of the quilt top; press.

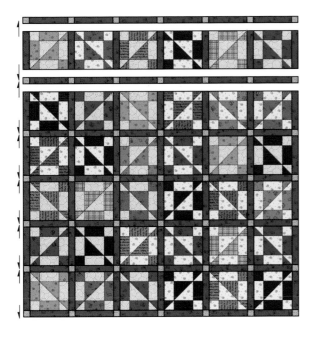

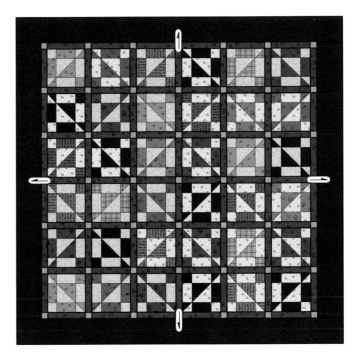

Adding the Borders

For detailed instructions, refer to "Borders with Overlapped Corners" on page 10.

1. Measure the quilt through the center from top to bottom and cut two border strips to fit that measurement.

2. Sew the trimmed border strips to the side edges of the quilt top. Press toward the border strips.

3. Measure the quilt through the center from side to side, including the borders just added. Cut two border strips to fit that measurement.

Finishing the Quilt

For detailed instructions on the following finishing techniques, refer to pages 13–17 of "Quiltmaking Basics."

1. Cut and piece the backing fabric so it is 4" to 6" larger than the quilt top. Layer the quilt top, batting, and backing; baste.

2. Hand or machine quilt as desired. Suggestions include machine quilting in the ditch along the blocks and sashing strips, and stipple quilting the border.

3. Square up the quilt sandwich.

4. Prepare and sew the binding to the quilt. Add a hanging sleeve, if desired, and a label.

DARGATE TRAILS

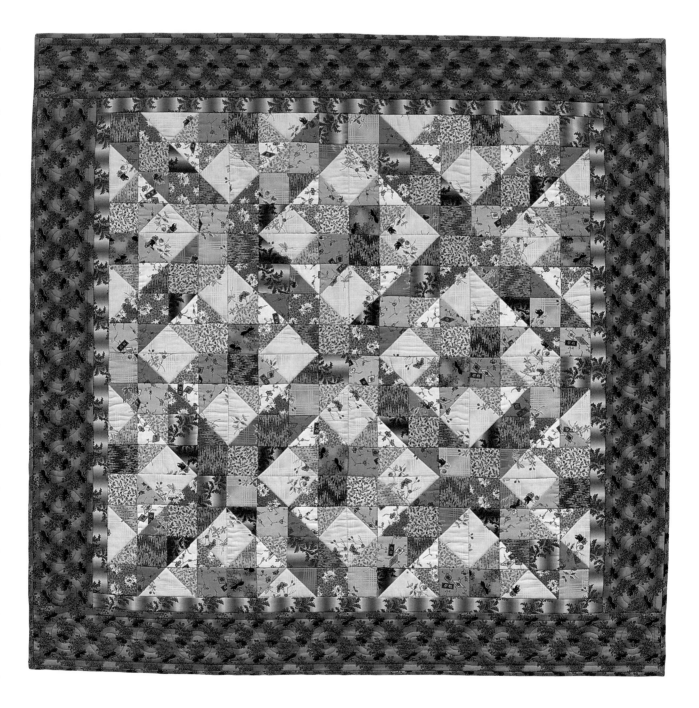

By Nancy Mahoney

From the collection of Clothworks, featuring their Dargate Divinity fabrics.

Finished Quilt Size: 42½" x 42½"

Finished Block Size: 8"

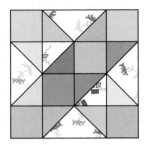

Side-by-side Free Trade blocks create this amazing quilt. The colors in the blocks are arranged so the green stars appear to float behind the pink lattice. Several values of pinks, greens, blues, and purples add interest and depth without adding difficulty.

Materials

Yardage is based on 42"-wide fabric.

1⅜ yards of pink print for blocks, outer border, and binding

¾ yard of background print A for blocks

⅜ yard of blue print for blocks and inner border

1 fat quarter of background print B for blocks

1 fat eighth (9" x 21") *each* of 5 blue prints for blocks

1 fat eighth *each* of 5 pink prints for blocks

1 fat eighth *each* of 4 purple prints for blocks

1 fat eighth *each* of 4 green prints for blocks

3 yards of fabric for backing

48" x 48" piece of batting

Cutting

All measurements include ¼" seam allowances. Unless otherwise noted, cut all strips from the crosswise grain. Outer (lengthwise) borders are cut long to allow for fabric shrinkage.

From the *lengthwise* grain of the 1⅜ yards of pink print, cut:
- 4 strips, 4½" x 49"
- 4 strips, 2" x 49"

From the remaining 1⅜ yards of pink print, cut:
- 1 square, 2⅞" x 2⅞"
- 9 squares, 2½" x 2½"

From *each* pink fat eighth, cut:
- 3 squares, 2⅞" x 2⅞" (15 total)
- 11 squares, 2½" x 2½" (55 total)

From background print B, cut:
- 16 squares, 2⅞" x 2⅞"

From *each* green fat eighth, cut:
- 16 squares, 2½" x 2½" (64 total)

From background print A, cut:
- 8 strips, 2½" x 42"; crosscut into 64 rectangles, 2½" x 4½"

From *each* blue fat eighth, cut:
- 11 squares, 2½" x 2½" (55 total)

From the ⅜ yard of blue print, cut:
- 4 strips, 1½" x 42"
- 9 squares, 2½" x 2½"

From *each* purple fat eighth, cut:
- 8 squares, 2½" x 2½" (32 total)

Making the Blocks

1. Using a pencil and ruler, draw a diagonal line from corner to corner on the wrong side of each background B square. Place a marked background square on a pink 2⅞" square, with right sides together and raw edges aligned. Stitch ¼" on either side of the diagonal line. Cut along

the drawn diagonal line to yield two half-square-triangle units; press. Make 32 units, 2½" x 2½".

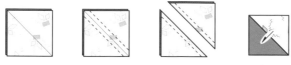

Make 32.

2. Refer to "Making Flying-Geese Units" on page 10. Stitch a pink 2½" square and a green 2½" square to a background A rectangle; press. Make 32 and label them unit A. Make 32, reversing the order of pink and green squares, and label them unit B.

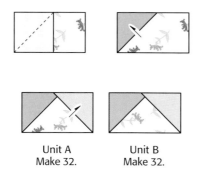

Unit A
Make 32.

Unit B
Make 32.

3. Sew two units from step 1 and two blue squares together as shown; press. Make 16 and label them unit C.

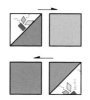

Unit C
Make 16.

4. Sew two each of unit A and unit B, a unit C, two blue squares, and two purple squares into rows as shown; press. Sew the rows together to complete the block; press. Make 16 blocks.

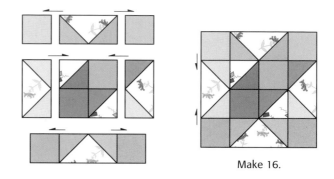

Make 16.

Assembling the Quilt Top

1. Arrange four blocks to make a row, rotating the blocks as shown. Sew the blocks together; press. Make four rows.

2. Sew the rows together; press.

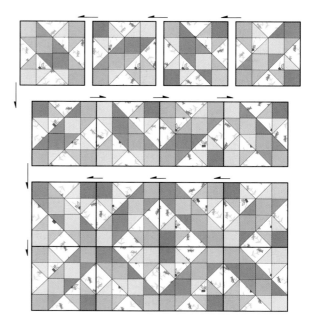

Adding the Borders

For detailed instructions, refer to "Borders with Overlapped Corners" on page 10.

1. Measure the quilt through the center from top to bottom and cut two inner-border strips to fit that measurement.

2. Sew the trimmed border strips to the side edges of the quilt top. Press toward the border strips.

3. Measure the quilt through the center from side to side, including the borders just added. Cut two inner-border strips to fit that measurement.

4. Sew the trimmed border strips to the top and bottom edges of the quilt top; press.

5. Repeat steps 1–4 to measure, trim, and add the outer-border strips. Press toward the outer-border strips.

Finishing the Quilt

For detailed instructions on the following finishing techniques, refer to pages 13–17 of "Quiltmaking Basics."

1. Cut and piece the backing fabric so it is 4" to 6" larger than the quilt top. Layer the quilt top, batting, and backing; baste.

2. Hand or machine quilt as desired. Suggestions include machine quilting in the ditch and quilting one of your favorite continuous-line designs in the borders.

3. Square up the quilt sandwich.

4. Prepare and sew the binding to the quilt. Add a hanging sleeve, if desired, and a label.

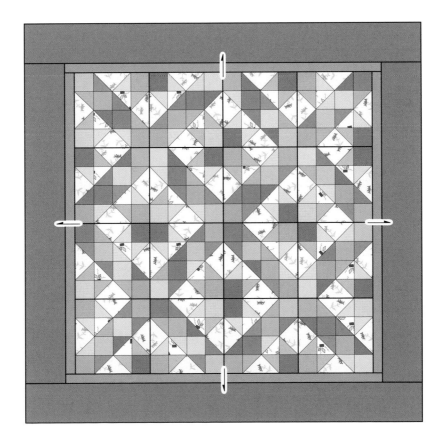

By Nancy Mahoney

From the collection of P & B Textiles, featuring their Pat L. Nickols fabrics.

Finished Quilt Size: 48½" x 48½"

Finished Block Size: 12"

Large-scale floral prints and a variety of fabrics give this quilt a wonderful scrappy look. Shortcut piecing techniques make constructing the blocks and sawtooth border a snap. Make your own version of this classic with a planned color scheme or one that's totally scrappy.

Materials

Yardage is based on 42"-wide fabric.

1¼ yards of red print for blocks and binding

⅝ yard *each* of 11 light prints for blocks, sashing, and border

½ yard *each* of green and navy prints for blocks

⅜ yard of green-and-black print for blocks and border

1 fat quarter *each* of blue and bright blue prints for blocks and border

1 fat quarter of red-and-black print for blocks, sashing squares, and border

1 fat quarter of medium-light floral print for sashing squares and border

1 fat quarter of medium-light tan print for blocks and border

1 fat quarter *each* of blue large-scale floral and green large-scale floral prints for blocks and border

1 fat eighth (9" x 21") of tan large-scale floral print for blocks

3¼ yards of fabric for backing

54" x 54" of batting

Cutting

All measurements include ¼" seam allowances. Cut all strips from the crosswise grain.

From *each* of the 11 light prints, cut:
- 2 squares, 8" x 8" (22 total)
- 1 strip, 2½" x 42" (11 total). Crosscut 6 strips into 7 squares each, 2½" x 2½" (42 total). Crosscut 5 strips into 6 squares each, 2½" x 2½" (30 total).
- 1 strip, 2½" x 42" (11 total). Crosscut 2 strips into 3 rectangles each, 2½" x 12½" (6 total). Crosscut 9 strips into 2 rectangles each, 2½" x 12½" (18 total).
- 1 strip, 2⅞" x 42" (11 total). Crosscut 3 strips into 4 squares each, 2⅞" x 2⅞" (12 total). Crosscut 8 strips into 3 squares cach, 2⅞" x 2⅞" (24 total). Cut all squares once diagonally to yield 72 triangles.

From the medium-light floral fat quarter, cut:
- 1 square, 8" x 8"
- 2 strips, 2½" x 21"; crosscut into 12 squares, 2½" x 2½"

From the medium-light tan fat quarter, cut:
- 3 squares, 8" x 8"

From the green-and-black print, cut:
- 1 strip, 2½" x 42"; crosscut into 12 squares, 2½" x 2½"
- 3 squares, 8" x 8"

From the blue fat quarter, cut:
- 4 squares, 8" x 8"

From the bright blue fat quarter, cut:
- 2 squares, 8" x 8"
- 2 strips, 2½" x 21"; crosscut into 12 squares, 2½" x 2½"

From the red-and-black fat quarter, cut:
- 1 square, 8" x 8"
- 2 strips, 2½" x 21"; crosscut into 16 squares, 2½" x 2½". Set 4 aside for sashing squares.

From the red print, cut:
- 6 strips, 2" x 42"
- 1 strip, 2½" x 42"; crosscut into 4 rectangles, 2½" x 4½"
- 3 strips, 8" x 42"; crosscut into 10 squares, 8" x 8"

From *each* green and navy print, cut:
- 2 squares, 8" x 8" (4 total)
- 2 strips, 2½" x 42" (4 total); crosscut each strip into 8 rectangles, 2½" x 4½" (32 total)

From *each* blue large-scale floral and green large-scale floral fat quarter, cut:
- 1 square, 8" x 8" (2 total)
- 3 squares, 6⅛" x 6⅛" (6 total)

From the tan large-scale floral fat eighth, cut:
- 3 squares, 6⅛" x 6⅛"

Making the Blocks

For detailed instructions, refer to "Half-Square-Triangle Units" on page 8 and "Making Flying-Geese Units" on page 10.

1. Pair each 8" light or medium-light print square with an 8" dark print square, right sides facing up. Cut and piece 2½"-wide bias strips to make 52 strip sets. Cut the strip sets to make 200 half-square-triangle units in matching sets of 4, each 2½" x 2½".

Make 52 strip sets.
Cut 200 units.

2. Sew two 2½" light squares to each 2½" x 4½" navy, green, and red print rectangle; press. Make 36.

Make 36.

3. Stitch two light 2⅞" triangles to a half-square-triangle unit from step 1; press. Make 36, in matching sets of 4.

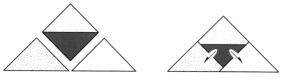

Make 36.

4. Fold a 6⅛" large-scale floral square in half vertically and horizontally, and lightly crease to mark the center of each side. Stitch matching triangle units from step 3 to opposite sides of the square, matching the center crease to the crossed seam of the triangle unit; press. Stitch matching triangle units to the remaining sides of the square; press. Make nine.

Make 9.

5. Stitch two units from step 1 to a unit from step 2; press. Make 36, in matching sets of 4.

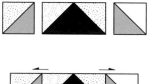

Make 36.

6. Sew a unit from step 4, four matching units from step 5, and four matching 2½" squares into rows as shown; press. Sew the rows to complete the block; press. Make nine blocks.

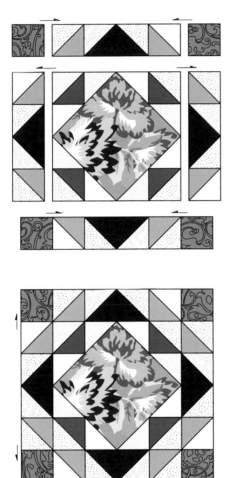

Make 9.

Assembling the Quilt Top

1. Sew three blocks and four 2½" x 12½" strips together to make a row; press. Make three rows and label them row A.

Row A
Make 3.

2. Sew three 2½" x 12½" strips and four 2½" medium-light floral squares together to make a row; press. Make two rows and label them row B.

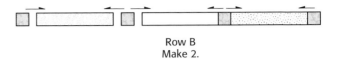

Row B
Make 2.

3. Sew three 2½" x 12½" strips, two 2½" red-and-black squares, and two 2½" medium-light floral squares together to make a row; press. Make two rows and label them row C.

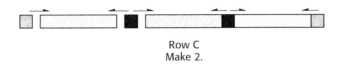

Row C
Make 2.

4. Sew the rows of blocks and sashing together as shown; press. Measure your quilt top; it should measure 44½" x 44½" (including seam allowance).

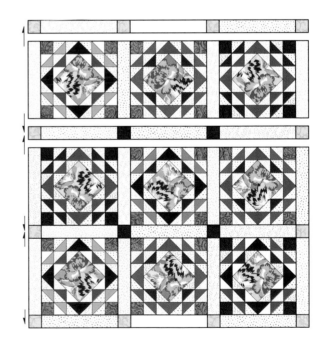

Adding the Borders

1. Sew 22 half-square-triangle units, turning them as shown, to make a side sawtooth border; press. Make two.

Make 2.

2. Sew 24 half-square-triangle units, turning them as shown, to make the top border; press. Repeat to make the bottom border.

Make 2.

3. Sew the side borders to the side edges of the quilt top; press.

4. Sew the top and bottom borders to the top and bottom edges of the quilt top; press.

Finishing the Quilt

For detailed instructions on the following finishing techniques, refer to pages 13–17 of "Quiltmaking Basics."

1. Cut and piece the backing fabric so it is 4" to 6" larger than the quilt top. Layer the quilt top, batting, and backing; baste.

2. Hand or machine quilt as desired. Suggestions include machine quilting in the ditch along the blocks, sashing strips, and sawtooth border.

3. Square up the quilt sandwich.

4. Prepare and sew the binding to the quilt. Add a hanging sleeve, if desired, and a label.

SPRING BOUQUET

By Nancy Mahoney

From the collection of P & B Textiles, featuring their Spring Mix fabrics.

Finished Quilt Size: 44½" x 44½"

Finished Block Size: 6"

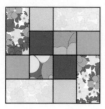

This bright and sunny quilt is simplicity itself! Three blue and three yellow prints are all it takes to make this uncomplicated design. You'll be pleased with how quickly the super-simple blocks, composed of rectangles and squares, go together.

Materials

Yardage is based on 42"-wide fabric.

1⅝ yards of yellow-and-blue large-scale floral print A for blocks and border

⅝ yard of dark blue print for blocks and binding

½ yard of yellow-and-blue large-scale floral print B for blocks

½ yard of yellow floral print for blocks

⅜ yard *each* of light blue and orange prints for blocks

2⅞ yards of fabric for backing

49" x 49" piece of batting

Cutting

All measurements include ¼" seam allowances. Unless otherwise noted, cut all strips from the crosswise grain. Outer (lengthwise) borders are cut long to allow for fabric shrinkage.

From the yellow-and-blue large-scale floral print A, cut:
- 4 strips, 2" x 42"

From the remaining *lengthwise* grain of the large-scale floral print A, cut:
- 4 strips, 4½" x 48"

From the dark blue print, cut:
- 9 strips, 2" x 42"

From *each* light blue and orange print, cut:
- 4 strips, 2" x 42" (8 total)

From the yellow-and-blue large-scale floral print B, cut:
- 7 strips, 2" x 42"; crosscut into 72 rectangles, 2" x 3½"

From the yellow floral print, cut:
- 7 strips, 2" x 42"; crosscut into 72 rectangles, 2" x 3½"

Making the Blocks

For detailed instructions, refer to "Making Strip Sets" on page 9.

1. Sew a light blue strip to a dark blue strip to make strip set A; press. Make four strip sets. Crosscut each strip set into 2" segments. Cut 72.

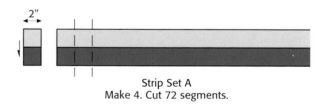

Strip Set A
Make 4. Cut 72 segments.

2. Repeat step 1 to sew an orange strip to a yellow-and-blue A strip to make strip set B; press. Make four strip sets. Crosscut each strip set into 2" segments. Cut 72.

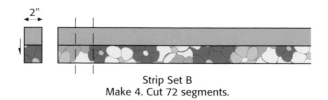

Strip Set B
Make 4. Cut 72 segments.

3. Sew each segment from step 1 to a yellow-and-blue B rectangle as shown; press. Make 72 and label them unit A.

Unit A
Make 72.

4. Sew each segment from step 2 to a yellow print rectangle as shown; press. Make 72 and label them unit B.

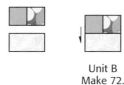

Unit B
Make 72.

5. Arrange and sew two A units and two B units into rows as shown; press. Sew the rows together to complete the block; press. Make 36.

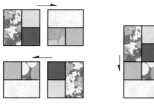

Make 36.

Assembling the Quilt Top

1. Arrange six rows of six blocks each, rotating them as shown. Sew the blocks together; press.

2. Sew the rows together; press.

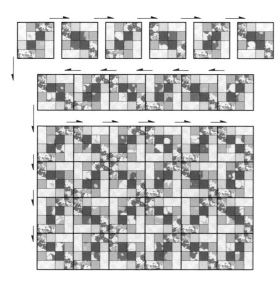

Adding the Borders

For detailed instructions, refer to "Borders with Overlapped Corners" on page 10.

1. Measure the quilt through the center from top to bottom and cut two border strips to fit that measurement.

2. Sew the trimmed border strips to the side edges of the quilt top. Press toward the border strips.

3. Measure the quilt through the center from side to side, including the borders just added. Cut two border strips to that measurement.

4. Sew the trimmed border strips to the top and bottom edges of the quilt top; press.

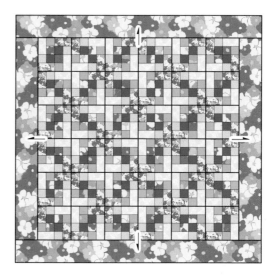

Finishing the Quilt

For detailed instructions on the following finishing techniques, refer to pages 13–17 of "Quiltmaking Basics."

1. Cut and piece the backing fabric so it is 4" to 6" larger than the quilt top. Layer the quilt top, batting, and backing; baste.

2. Hand or machine quilt as desired. Suggestions include machine quilting in the ditch, quilting a single chain on the diagonal across the blue squares, and stipple quilting the border.

3. Square up the quilt sandwich.

4. Prepare and sew the binding to the quilt. Add a hanging sleeve, if desired, and a label.

By Nancy Mahoney

From the collection of P & B Textiles, featuring their Spring Fling fabrics.

Finished Quilt Size: 47½" x 56½"

Finished Block Size: 9"

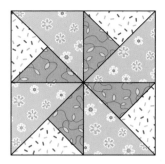

The traditional 1930s Whirligig block is paired with wonderful, whimsical floral prints to make this fun and easy quilt. (Each block uses only three fabrics!) The playful design is sure to bring out a smile, and makes an ideal choice for a child's quilt.

Materials

Yardage is based on 42"-wide fabric.

1½ yards of blue floral print for blocks and outer border

¾ yard of pink small-scale print for blocks and inner border

¾ yard of light background print for blocks

⅝ yard of dark blue small-scale print for blocks and binding

½ yard *each* of yellow, blue, and green button-flowers print for blocks

1 fat quarter *each* of green, yellow, light blue, and grape small-scale prints for blocks

3⅛ yards of fabric for backing

52" x 62" piece of batting

Cutting

All measurements include ¼" seam allowances. Unless otherwise noted, cut all strips from the crosswise grain. Outer (lengthwise) borders are cut long to allow for fabric shrinkage.

From the light background print, cut:
- 20 squares, 5¾" x 5¾"; cut twice diagonally to yield 80 triangles

From the pink small-scale print, cut:
- 5 strips, 1½" x 42"
- 4 squares, 5¾" x 5¾"; cut twice diagonally to yield 16 triangles

From the dark blue small-scale print, cut:
- 3 squares, 5¾" x 5¾"; cut twice diagonally to yield 12 triangles
- 6 strips, 2" x 42"

From *each* green, yellow, and light blue small-scale print fat quarter, cut:
- 3 squares, 5¾" x 5¾" (9 total); cut twice diagonally to yield 36 triangles

From the grape small-scale print fat quarter, cut:
- 4 squares, 5¾" x 5¾"; cut twice diagonally to yield 16 triangles

From the *lengthwise* grain of the blue floral print, cut:
- 4 strips, 5" x 54"
- 10 squares, 5⅜" x 5⅜"; cut once diagonally to yield 20 triangles

From the yellow button-flowers print, cut:
- 8 squares, 5⅜" x 5⅜"; cut once diagonally to yield 16 triangles

From the blue button-flowers print, cut:
- 10 squares, 5⅜" x 5⅜"; cut once diagonally to yield 20 triangles

From the green button-flowers print, cut:
- 12 squares, 5⅜" x 5⅜"; cut once diagonally to yield 24 triangles

Making the Blocks

1. Stitch each background triangle to a small-scale print triangle to make a triangle unit; press. Make 80, in matching sets of 4.

Make 80.

2. Sew each unit from step 1 to a blue floral or button-flower triangle; press. Make 80, in matching sets of 4.

Make 80.

3. Sew four matching units from step 2 into rows, rotating the units as shown; press. Sew the rows together to complete the block; press. Make 20 blocks.

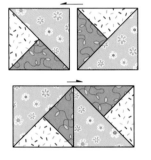
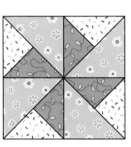

Make 20.

Assembling the Quilt Top

1. Arrange and sew the blocks in five rows of four blocks each; press.

2. Sew the rows together; press.

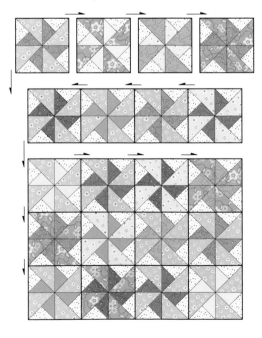

Adding the Borders

For detailed instructions, refer to "Borders with Overlapped Corners" on page 10.

1. Sew three inner-border strips end to end to make a continuous strip. Measure the quilt through the center from top to bottom and cut two border strips to fit that measurement.

2. Sew the trimmed border strips to the side edges of the quilt top. Press toward the border strips.

3. Measure the quilt through the center from side to side, including the borders just added. Cut the remaining two inner-border strips to fit that measurement.

4. Sew the trimmed border strips to the top and bottom edges of the quilt top; press.

5. Repeat steps 1–4 to measure, trim, and add the outer-border strips. (You will not need to piece the strips.) Press toward the outer-border strips.

Finishing the Quilt

For detailed instructions on the following finishing techniques, refer to pages 13–17 of "Quiltmaking Basics."

1. Cut and piece the backing fabric so it is 4" to 6" larger than the quilt top. Layer the quilt top, batting, and backing; baste.

2. Hand or machine quilt as desired. Suggestions include machine quilting in the ditch and stipple quilting the border.

3. Square up the quilt sandwich.

4. Prepare and sew the binding to the quilt. Add a hanging sleeve, if desired, and a label.

LEMON KRYSTALS

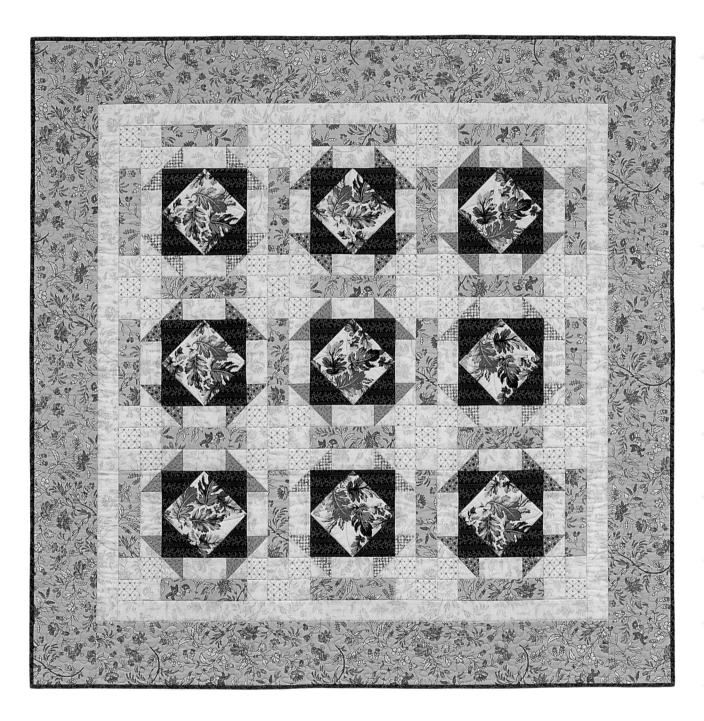

By Nancy Mahoney
From the collection of P & B Textiles, featuring their Krystal Lilies fabrics.

Finished Quilt Size: 45½" x 45½"

Finished Block Size: 9"

Blue and yellow make a winning combination in this marvelous quilt. Each block center features a theme print, and a light blue print adds interest and transparency. The combination of blocks and pieced sashing creates a quilt that seems complex but is really quite simple to make.

Materials

Yardage is based on 42"-wide fabric.

1½ yards of blue floral print for sashing and outer border

1¼ yards of light yellow print for blocks, sashing, and inner border

⅝ yard of dark blue print for blocks and binding

¼ yard of light blue print for blocks and sashing squares

1 fat quarter *each* of 3 blue prints for blocks

1 fat quarter of yellow-and-blue leaf print for blocks

2⅞ yards of fabric for backing

50" x 50" piece of batting

Cutting

All measurements include ¼" seam allowances. Unless otherwise noted, cut all strips from the crosswise grain. Outer (lengthwise) borders are cut long to allow for fabric shrinkage.

From the light yellow print, cut:
- 3 rectangles, 9" x 20"
- 4 strips, 2" x 42"; crosscut into 36 rectangles, 2" x 3½"
- 3 strips, 2" x 42"; crosscut into 48 squares, 2" x 2"
- 4 strips, 2" x 42"

From *each* blue print fat quarter, cut:
- 1 rectangle, 9" x 20" (3 total)

From the yellow-and-blue leaf print, cut:
- 9 squares, 4¾" x 4¾"

From the dark blue print, cut:
- 2 strips, 3⅞" x 42"; crosscut into 18 squares, 3⅞" x 3⅞". Cut once diagonally to yield 36 triangles.

From the light blue print, cut:
- 3 strips, 2" x 42"; crosscut into 52 squares, 2" x 2"

From the *lengthwise* grain of the blue floral print, cut:
- 4 strips, 5" x 54"
- 3 strips, 2" x 54"; crosscut into 24 rectangles, 2" x 6½"

Making the Blocks

For detailed instructions, refer to "Half-Square-Triangle Units" on page 8.

1. Pair each 9" x 20" light yellow rectangle with a 9" x 20" blue print rectangle, right sides facing up. Cut and piece 2½"-wide bias strips to make six strip sets. Cut the strip sets to make 72 half-square-triangle units in matching sets of 8, each 2" x 2".

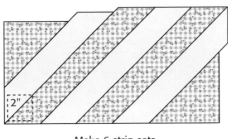

Make 6 strip sets.
Cut 72 units.

2. Fold a leaf print square in half vertically and horizontally, and lightly crease to mark the center of each side. Fold four dark blue triangles in half, and lightly crease to mark the center of the long side. Stitch triangles to opposite sides of the square, matching the center creases; press. Stitch triangles to the remaining sides of the square; press. Make nine.

Make 9.

3. Sew a unit from step 2, four light blue squares, four light yellow 2" x 3½" rectangles, and eight matching units from step 1 into rows as shown; press. Stitch the rows together to complete the block; press. Make nine blocks.

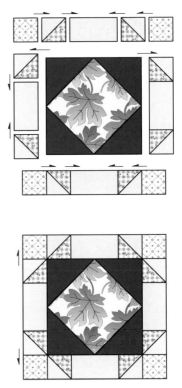

Make 9.

Assembling the Quilt Top

1. Sew two light yellow squares and one blue floral rectangle to make a sashing unit; press. Make 24.

Make 24.

2. Sew three blocks and four sashing units together to make a row; press. Make three rows.

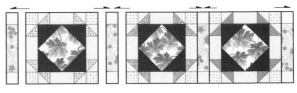

Make 3.

3. Sew four light blue squares and three sashing units together to make a sashing row; press. Make four rows.

Make 4.

4. Sew the rows of blocks and sashing together; press.

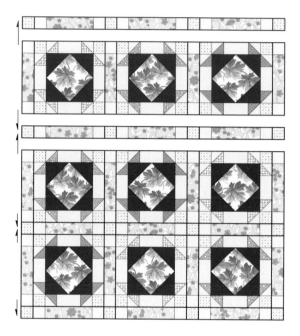

Adding the Borders

For detailed instructions, refer to "Borders with Overlapped Corners" on page 10.

1. Measure the quilt through the center from top to bottom and cut two inner-border strips to fit that measurement.

2. Sew the trimmed border strips to the side edges of the quilt top. Press toward the border strips.

3. Measure the quilt through the center from side to side, including the borders just added. Cut the remaining two inner-border strips to fit that measurement.

4. Sew the trimmed border strips to the top and bottom edges of the quilt top; press.

5. Repeat steps 1–4 to measure, trim, and add the outer-border strips. Press toward the outer-border strips.

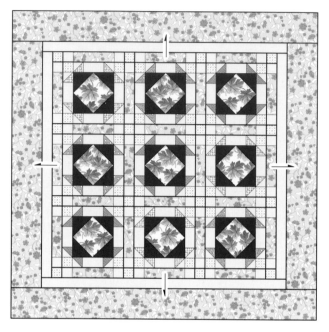

Finishing the Quilt

For detailed instructions on the following finishing techniques, refer to pages 13–17 of "Quiltmaking Basics."

1. Cut and piece the backing fabric so it is 4" to 6" larger than the quilt top. Layer the quilt top, batting, and backing; baste.

2. Hand or machine quilt as desired. Suggestions include machine quilting in the ditch and stipple quilting the border.

3. Square up the quilt sandwich.

4. Prepare and sew the binding to the quilt. Add a hanging sleeve, if desired, and a label.

ROMANCING THE BLUES

By Nancy Mahoney

From the collection of P & B Textiles, featuring their Redwork Romance fabrics.

Finished Quilt Size: 40¾" x 50½"

Finished Block Size: 9¾"

Blue and white is an all-time favorite color combination for quilts, and shortcut techniques make stitching this one a breeze. This charming quilt showcases a theme print—cut from a printed panel with designs reminiscent of redwork—in the center of each block. A large-scale floral print or fun novelty print makes an excellent alternative.

Materials

Yardage is based on 42"-wide fabric.

1½ yards of blue print for blocks, inner and outer borders, and binding

¾ yard of light background theme print for blocks*

⅜ yard of blue-and-white stripe for middle border

1 fat quarter *each* of 4 light background prints for blocks

1 fat quarter *each* of 3 blue prints for blocks

3 yards of fabric for backing

45" x 55" piece of batting

* *The motifs in the theme print were "fussy cut" to feature specific areas of the fabric. If you plan to fussy cut, you may need to purchase extra fabric.*

Cutting

All measurements include ¼" seam allowances. Unless otherwise noted, cut all strips from the crosswise grain. Outer (lengthwise) borders are cut long to allow for fabric shrinkage.

From *each* light background fat quarter, cut:
  ❖ 1 rectangle, 18" x 21" (4 total)

From the *lengthwise* grain of the 1½ yards of blue print, cut:
  ❖ 4 strips, 3½" x 54"
  ❖ 8 strips, 2" x 54"
  ❖ 1 rectangle, 18" x 21"

From *each* blue print fat quarter, cut:
  ❖ 1 rectangle, 18" x 21" (3 total)

From the light background theme print, cut:
  ❖ 12 squares, 7" x 7"

From the blue-and-white stripe, cut:
  ❖ 5 strips, 1½" x 42"

Making the Blocks

For detailed instructions, refer to "Half-Square-Triangle Units" on page 8.

1. Pair each 18" x 21" background print rectangle with an 18" x 21" blue print rectangle, right sides facing up. Cut and piece 2¼"-wide bias strips to make eight strip sets. Cut the strip sets into 240 half-square-triangle units, each 2⅛" x 2⅛".

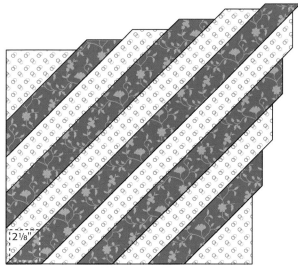

Make 8 strip sets.
Cut 240 units.

2. Sew four units from step 1 together, rotating them as shown; press. Make 24.

Make 24.

3. Sew six units from step 1 together, rotating them as shown; press. Make 24.

Make 24.

4. Sew a theme print square, two units from step 2, and two units from step 3 together as shown to complete the block; press. Make 12 blocks.

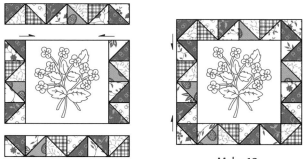

Make 12.

Assembling the Quilt Top

1. Arrange and sew the blocks in four rows of three blocks each; press.

2. Sew the rows together; press.

Adding the Borders

For detailed instructions, refer to "Borders with Overlapped Corners" on page 10.

1. Measure the quilt through the center from top to bottom and cut two 2"-wide blue print strips to fit that measurement.

2. Sew the trimmed inner-border strips to the side edges of the quilt top. Press toward the border strips.

3. Measure the quilt through the center from side to side, including the borders just added. Cut two 2"-wide blue print strips to fit that measurement.

4. Sew the trimmed inner-border strips to the top and bottom edges of the quilt top; press.

5. Join three blue-and-white stripe strips end to end to make a continuous strip. Measure the quilt through the center from top to bottom and cut two middle-border strips to fit that measurement.

6. Sew the trimmed strips to the side edges of the quilt top; press.

7. Measure the quilt from side to side, including the borders just added. Cut the remaining two middle-border strips to fit that measurement.

8. Sew the trimmed border strips to the top and bottom edges of the quilt top; press.

9. Repeat steps 1–4 to measure, trim, and add the 3½"-wide blue outer-border strips. Press toward the outer-border strips.

Finishing the Quilt

For detailed instructions on the following finishing techniques, refer to pages 13–17 of "Quiltmaking Basics."

1. Cut and piece the backing fabric so it is 4" to 6" larger than the quilt top. Layer the quilt top, batting, and backing; baste.

2. Hand or machine quilt as desired. Suggestions include machine quilting in the ditch around the blocks and border, quilting the center motif following the lines of the fabric, and quilting the outer border with wavy lines.

3. Square up the quilt sandwich.

4. Prepare and sew the binding to the quilt. Add a hanging sleeve, if desired, and a label.

Helpful Tip

For a scrappy look, pair each 18" x 21" blue print rectangle with an 18" x 21" background rectangle, right sides facing up, and cut into bias strips. Mix and match the bias strips, alternating the blue prints and the background prints, to form a rectangle. Arrange and sew the strips by size; the sewn unit should have two even and two uneven sides.

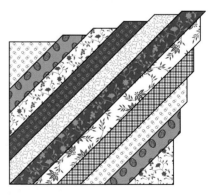

INDIGO CHAIN

By Nancy Mahoney

From the collection of P & B Textiles, featuring their Vintage Indigos fabrics.

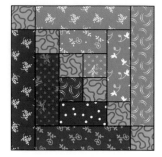

Finished Quilt Size: 47½" x 47½"

Finished Block Size: 9"

This quilt uses reproduction fabrics in a stunning variation of a traditional pattern. The quick and easy Cornerstone blocks are arranged to create a secondary star pattern. Follow a planned color scheme to make your own version of this classic, or try a totally scrappy palette for a charming addition to any country-style decor.

Materials

Yardage is based on 42"-wide fabric.

1½ yards of navy print for blocks, outer border, and binding

⅝ yard of pink print for blocks and inner border

1 fat quarter *each* of 8 light blue prints for blocks

1 fat quarter *each* of 7 navy blue prints for blocks

3 yards of fabric for backing

52" x 52" piece of batting

Cutting

All measurements include ¼" seam allowances. Unless otherwise noted, cut all strips from the crosswise grain. Outer (lengthwise) borders are cut long to allow for fabric shrinkage.

From the pink print, cut:
- 4 strips, 2" x 42"
- 5 strips, 2" x 42"; crosscut into 96 squares, 2" x 2"

From *each* light blue fat quarter, cut:
- 2 squares, 2" x 2" (16 total)
- 2 rectangles, 2" x 3½" (16 total)
- 2 rectangles, 2" x 5" (16 total)
- 2 rectangles, 2" x 6½" (16 total)
- 2 rectangles, 2" x 8" (16 total)

From the *lengthwise* grain of the 1½ yards of navy print, cut:
- 4 strips, 4½" x 54"
- 4 strips, 2" x 54"

From the remaining 1½ yards of navy print, cut:
- 2 squares, 2" x 2"
- 2 rectangles, 2" x 3½"
- 2 rectangles, 2" x 5"
- 2 rectangles, 2" x 6½"
- 2 rectangles, 2" x 8"

From *each* navy blue fat quarter, cut:
- 2 squares, 2" x 2" (14 total)
- 2 rectangles, 2" x 3½" (14 total)
- 2 rectangles, 2" x 5" (14 total)
- 2 rectangles, 2" x 6½" (14 total)
- 2 rectangles, 2" x 8" (14 total)

Making the Blocks

1. Sew each light blue square to a pink square. Sew each navy blue square to a pink square; press. Sew one of each unit together to make a four-patch unit; press. Make 16.

Make 16.

2. Sew a light blue 2" x 3½" rectangle and a navy blue 2" x 3½" rectangle to opposite sides of each unit from step 1 as shown; press. Make 16.

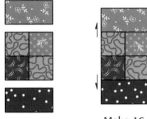

Make 16.

3. Sew a pink square to a light blue 2" x 5" rectangle; press. Make 16. Sew a pink square to a navy blue 2" x 5" rectangle; press. Make 16. Sew one of each to opposite sides of each unit from step 2 as shown; press. Make 16.

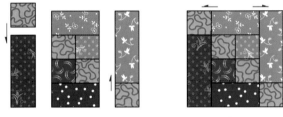

Make 16.

4. Sew a light blue 2" x 6½" rectangle and a navy blue 2" x 6½" rectangle to opposite sides of each unit from step 3 as shown; press. Make 16.

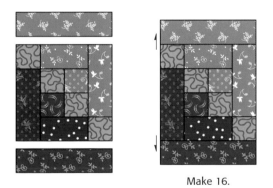

Make 16.

5. Sew a pink square to a light blue 2" x 8" rectangle; press. Make 16. Sew a pink square to a navy blue 2" x 8" rectangle; press. Make 16. Sew one of each to opposite sides of each unit from step 4 as

shown to complete the block; press. Make 16 blocks.

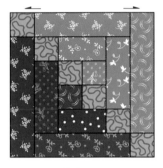

Make 16.

Assembling the Quilt Top

1. Arrange and sew the blocks in four rows of four blocks each, rotating the blocks as shown; press.

2. Sew the rows together; press.

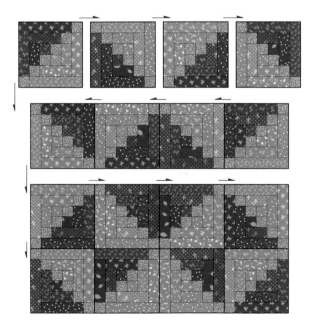

Adding the Borders

For detailed instructions, refer to "Borders with Overlapped Corners" on page 10 as needed.

1. Measure the quilt through the center from top to bottom and cut two inner-border strips to fit that measurement.

2. Sew the trimmed border strips to the side edges of the quilt top. Press toward the border strips.

3. Measure the quilt through the center from side to side, including the borders just added. Cut two inner-border strips to fit that measurement.

4. Sew the trimmed border strips to the top and bottom edges of the quilt top; press.

5. Repeat steps 1–4 to measure, trim, and add the outer-border strips. Press toward the outer-border strips.

Finishing the Quilt

For detailed instructions on the following finishing techniques, refer to pages 13–17 of "Quiltmaking Basics."

1. Cut and piece the backing fabric so it is 4" to 6" larger than the quilt top. Layer the quilt top, batting, and backing; baste.

2. Hand or machine quilt as desired. Suggestions include machine quilting with straight lines on the diagonal through the pink squares and free-motion quilting a stipple design over the blocks and in the outer border.

3. Square up the quilt sandwich.

4. Prepare and sew the binding to the quilt. Add a hanging sleeve, if desired, and a label.

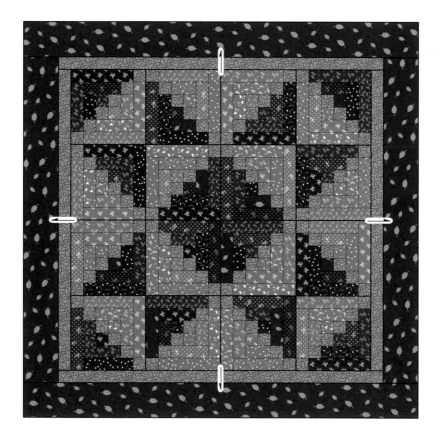

STAR BABIES

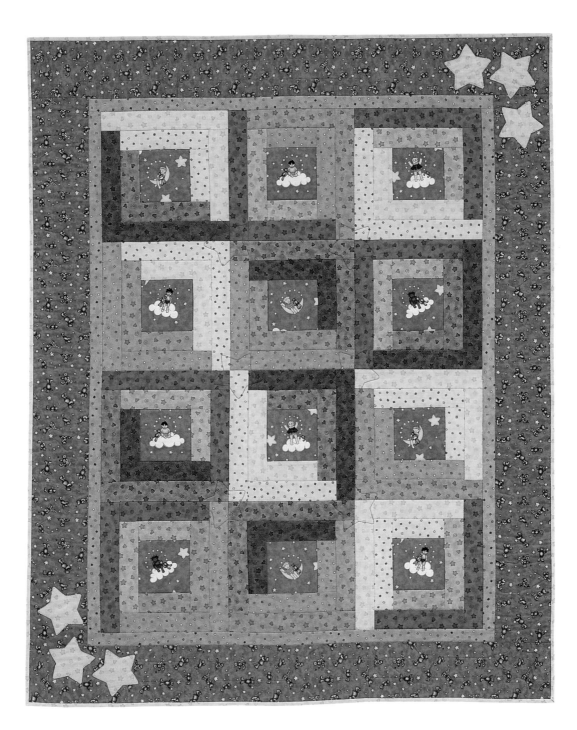

By Nancy Mahoney

From the collection of P & B Textiles, featuring their Buddy and the Starbabies fabrics.

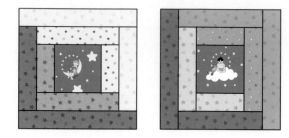

Finished Quilt Size: 41½" x 51½"

Finished Block Size: 10"

This cheerful quilt adds a bright spot to any child's room. The Courthouse Steps blocks are simple to stitch, and the block center is ideal for a favorite novelty print. Charming appliquéd stars add to the sparkling "personality" of this playful quilt.

Materials

Yardage is based on 42"-wide fabric.

1⅜ yards of blue bear print for outer border

⅞ yard of yellow tone-on-tone print for blocks, appliqués, and binding

⅜ yard of theme or novelty print for blocks*

⅜ yard *each* of dark blue, light blue, purple, violet, and turquoise tone-on-tone prints for blocks

⅜ yard *each* of turquoise-with-boxes and yellow-with-boxes prints for blocks

¼ yard of green print for inner border

3 yards of fabric for backing

45" x 55" piece of batting

⅛ yard of lightweight fusible web

* The motifs in the novelty print were "fussy cut" to feature specific areas of the fabric. If you plan to fussy cut, you may need to purchase extra fabric.

Cutting

All measurements include ¼" seam allowances. Unless otherwise noted, cut all strips from the crosswise grain. Outer (lengthwise) borders are cut long to allow for fabric shrinkage.

From the yellow tone-on-tone print, cut:
- 5 strips, 2" x 42"
- 3 rectangles, 2" x 4½"
- 6 rectangles, 2" x 7½"
- 3 rectangles, 2" x 10½"

From the light blue tone-on-tone print, cut:
- 6 rectangles, 2" x 4½"
- 6 rectangles, 2" x 7½"

From *each* purple, violet, and turquoise tone-on-tone print, cut:
- 3 rectangles, 2" x 4½" (9 total)
- 6 rectangles, 2" x 7½" (18 total)
- 3 rectangles, 2" x 10½" (9 total)

From *each* turquoise-with-boxes and yellow-with-boxes print, cut:
- 3 rectangles, 2" x 4½" (6 total)
- 6 rectangles, 2" x 7½" (12 total)
- 3 rectangles, 2" x 10½" (6 total)

From the theme or novelty print, cut:
- 12 squares, 4½" x 4½"

From the dark blue tone-on-tone print, cut:
- 6 rectangles, 2" x 7½"
- 6 rectangles, 2" x 10½"

From the green print, cut:
- 4 strips, 1½" x 42"

From the *lengthwise* grain of the blue bear print, cut:
- 4 strips, 5" x 49"

Making the Blocks

1. Sew two different 2" x 4½" rectangles to opposite sides of a novelty square; press. Make six and label them unit A. Sew two different 2" x 4½" rectangles to the top and bottom of each remaining novelty square; press. Make six and label them unit B.

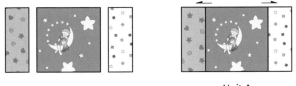

Unit A
Make 6.

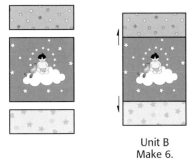

Unit B
Make 6.

2. Sew 2" x 7½" rectangles in the same colors to the top and bottom of each unit A from step 1; press. Make six and label them unit A. Sew 2" x 7½" rectangles in the same colors to the sides of each unit B; press. Make six and label them unit B.

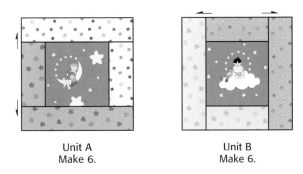

Unit A
Make 6.

Unit B
Make 6.

3. Sew two different 2" x 7½" rectangles to opposite sides of each unit A from step 2; press. Make six and label them unit A. Sew two different 2" x 7½" rectangles to the top and bottom of

each unit B from step 2; press. Make six and label them unit B.

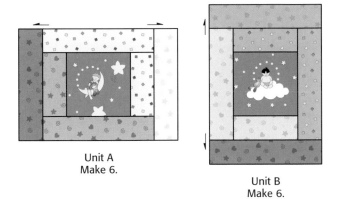

Unit A
Make 6.

Unit B
Make 6.

4. Sew 2" x 10½" rectangles in the same colors to the top and bottom of each unit A from step 3 to complete the block; press. Make six and label them block A. Sew 2" x 10½" rectangles in the same colors to the sides of each unit B from step 3 to complete the block; press. Make six and label them block B.

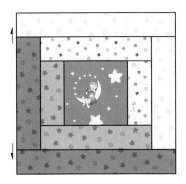

Block A
Make 6.

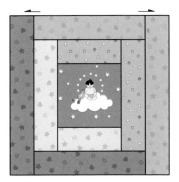

Block B
Make 6.

Assembling the Quilt Top

1. Arrange and sew the blocks in four rows of three blocks each, alternating A and B blocks as shown; press.

2. Sew the rows together; press.

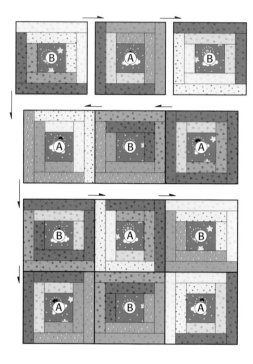

Adding the Borders

For detailed instructions, refer to "Borders with Overlapped Corners" on page 10.

1. Join the inner-border strips end to end to make a continuous strip. Measure the quilt through the center from top to bottom and cut two border strips to fit that measurement.

2. Sew the trimmed border strips to the side edges of the quilt top. Press toward the border strips.

3. Measure the quilt through the center from side to side, including the borders just added. Cut two border strips to fit that measurement.

4. Sew the trimmed border strips to the top and bottom edges of the quilt top; press.

5. Repeat steps 1–4 to measure, trim, and add the outer-border strips. (You will not need to piece the strips.) Press toward the outer-border strips.

Appliquéing the Border

1. Use the pattern below to make a template for the star appliqué. Follow the manufacturer's instructions to trace six stars onto fusible web, and fuse to the wrong side of the remaining yellow tone-on-tone fabric. Cut out the stars. Fuse the stars to the outer border of the quilt top as shown in the quilt photo on page 65.

2. Use matching-colored thread to appliqué the stars using a straight, zigzag, or buttonhole stitch.

Finishing the Quilt

For detailed instructions on the following finishing techniques, refer to pages 13–17 of "Quiltmaking Basics."

1. Cut and piece the backing fabric so it is 4" to 6" larger than the quilt top. Layer the quilt top, batting, and backing; baste.

2. Hand or machine quilt as desired. Suggestions include machine quilting in the ditch in blocks and borders, and quilting stars at the intersection of four blocks and in the outer border.

3. Square up the quilt sandwich.

4. Prepare and sew the binding to the quilt. Add a hanging sleeve, if desired, and a label.

Star
Cut 6.

Pattern does not include seam allowance.

FUNNY FARM

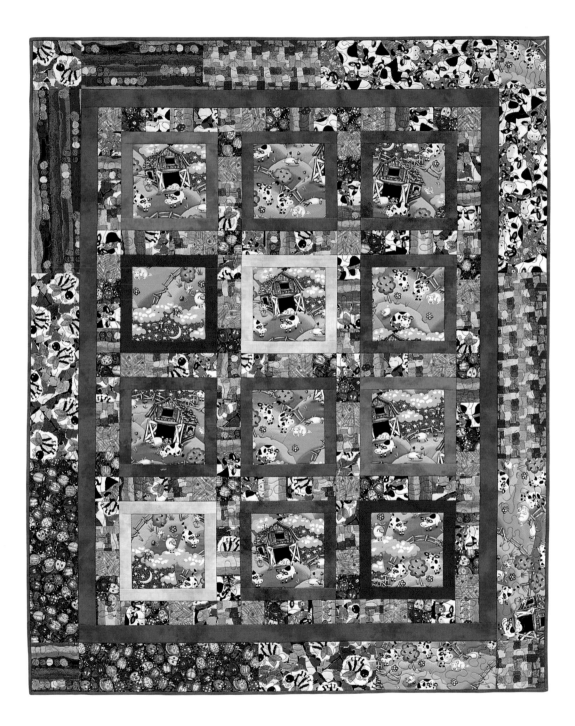

By Nancy Mahoney

From the collection of Timeless Treasures, featuring their Novelty fabrics.

Finished Quilt Size: 43½" x 53½"

Finished Block Size: 8"

This clever quilt—a great choice for a child—makes an ideal showcase for novelty prints. The blocks zoom together in no time, and the colorful pieced sashing, which may look complex, is really simple and fun to make.

Materials

Yardage is based on 42"-wide fabric.

⅞ yard of blue marbled solid for blocks, inner border, and binding

⅝ yard of farm-scene print for blocks and outer border*

⅜ yard *each* of 5 novelty prints for sashing and outer border

¼ yard of green print for sashing

1 fat quarter *each* of red, orange, yellow, green, and purple marbled solids for blocks

3 yards of fabric for backing

48" x 58" piece of batting

* *The block centers in the farm-scene print were "fussy cut" to feature specific motifs. If you plan to fussy cut, you may need to purchase extra fabric.*

Cutting

All measurements include ¼" seam allowances. Cut all strips from the crosswise grain.

From the blue marbled solid, cut:

- 11 strips, 2" x 42"
- 2 strips, 1½" x 42"; crosscut into 4 rectangles, 1½" x 8½"; and 4 rectangles, 1½" x 6½"

From *each* marbled-solid fat quarter, cut:

- 4 strips, 1½" x 20" (20 total); crosscut into 4 rectangles, 1½" x 8½" (20 total); and 4 rectangles, 1½" x 6½" (20 total)

From the farm-scene print, cut:

- 1 strip, 4½" x 42"; crosscut into 1 rectangle, 4½" x 15½"; 1 rectangle, 4½" x 10½"; and 1 square, 4½" x 4½"
- 12 squares, 6½" x 6½"

From *each* of 3 novelty prints, cut:

- 2 strips, 2½" x 42" (6 total); crosscut each into 2 strips, 2½" x 20"
- 1 strip, 4½" x 42" (3 total); crosscut each into 1 rectangle, 4½" x 15½"; 1 rectangle, 4½" x 10½"; and 1 square, 4½" x 4½"

From *each* remaining novelty print, cut:

- 2 strips, 2½" x 42" (4 total); crosscut each into 2 strips, 2½" x 20"
- 1 strip, 4½" x 42" (2 total); crosscut into 2 rectangles, 4½" x 15½"

From the green print, cut:

- 2 strips, 2½" x 42"; crosscut each into 2 strips, 2½" x 20"

Making the Blocks

1. Sew matching 1½" x 6½" rectangles to opposite sides of each 6½" square; press. Make 12.

Make 12.

2. Sew matching 1½" x 8½" rectangles to the remaining sides of the unit from step 1; press. Make 12.

Make 12.

Assembling the Quilt Top

For detailed instructions, refer to "Making Strip Sets" on page 9.

1. Randomly combine and sew four 2½" x 20" strips together to make a strip set; press. Make a total of five strip sets, randomly combining the fabrics in each. (You'll have a few strips left over.) Crosscut each strip set into 2½" segments. Cut 36 for sashing units.

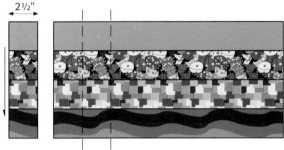

Make 5 strip sets.
Cut 36 segments.

2. Sew three blocks and four sashing units together to make a row; press. Make four rows.

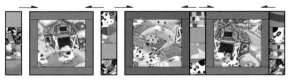

Make 4.

3. Randomly combine and sew four sashing units end to end to make a row; press. Make five rows.

Make 5.

4. Sew the rows of blocks and sashing together, re-pressing seams in sashing rows as needed to create opposing seams.

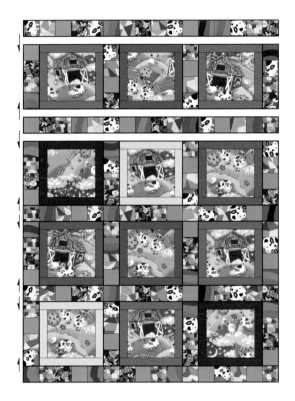

Adding the Borders

For detailed instructions, refer to "Borders with Overlapped Corners" on page 10 and "Borders with Corner Squares" on page 11.

1. Join three inner-border strips end to end to make a continuous strip. Measure the quilt through the center from top to bottom and cut two inner-border strips to fit that measurement.

2. Sew the trimmed border strips to the side edges of the quilt top. Press toward the border strips.

3. Measure the quilt through the center from side to side, including the borders just added. Cut the remaining two inner-border strips to fit that measurement.

4. Sew the trimmed border strips to the top and bottom edges of the quilt top; press.

5. Randomly combine and sew three 4½" x 15½" rectangles end to end to make a side outer-border strip; press. Make two.

Make 2.

6. Randomly combine and sew two 4½" x 10½" rectangles and a 4½" x 15½" rectangle end to end to make the top-border strip as shown; press. Repeat to make the bottom-border strip.

Make 2.

7. Sew the side outer-border strips from step 5 to the side edges of the quilt top. Press toward the outer-border strips.

8. Sew a 4½" square to each end of the top and bottom outer-border strips; press.

9. Sew the border strips from step 8 to the top and bottom edges of the quilt top; press.

Finishing the Quilt

For detailed instructions on the following finishing techniques, refer to pages 13–17 of "Quiltmaking Basics."

1. Cut and piece the backing fabric so it is 4" to 6" larger than the quilt top. Layer the quilt top, batting, and backing; baste.

2. Hand or machine quilt as desired. Suggestions include machine quilting in the ditch along the sashing strips, borders, and around the center square of each block; quilting along the lines of the fabric in the center squares; and stipple quilting the sashing strips and outer border.

3. Square up the quilt sandwich.

4. Prepare and sew the binding to the quilt. Add a hanging sleeve, if desired, and a label.

GEOMEX STARS

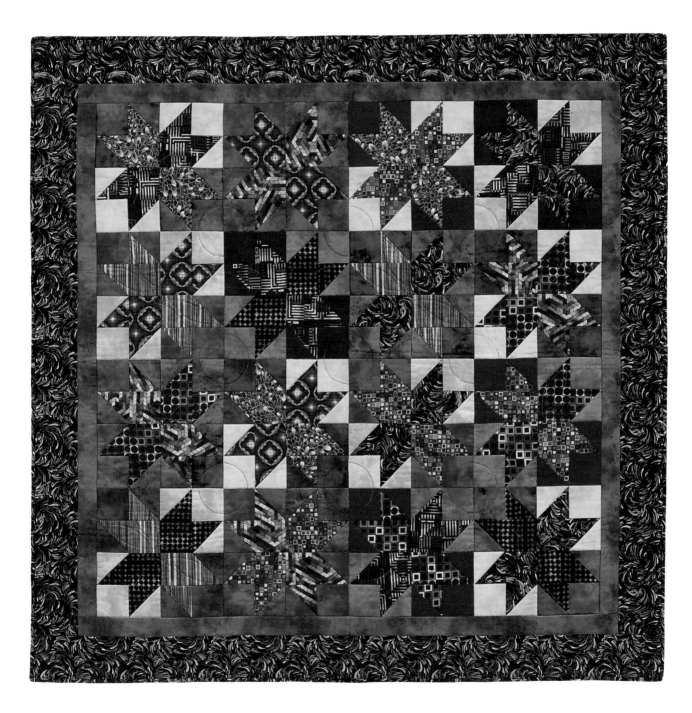

By Nancy Mahoney

From the collection of Timeless Treasures, featuring their Geomex and Marble Mania fabrics.

Finished Quilt Size: 50½" x 50½"

Finished Block Size: 10"

The combination of marbled solids and bright geometric prints creates a sophisticated quilt sure to add pizzazz to any decor. The simple Spinning Star blocks are constructed of squares and rectangles—no fussing with triangles. Have fun!

Materials

Yardage is based on 42"-wide fabric.

1⅝ yards of multicolored geometric print for blocks, outer border, and binding

¾ yard of grape marbled solid for blocks and inner border

1 fat quarter *each* of 8 multicolored geometric prints for blocks

1 fat quarter *each* of lemon, orange, light blue, dark blue, cherry, dark green, violet, and lime green marbled solids for blocks

3⅜ yards of fabric for backing

55" x 55" piece of batting

Cutting

All measurements include ¼" seam allowances. Unless otherwise noted, cut all strips from the crosswise grain. Outer (lengthwise) borders are cut long to allow for fabric shrinkage.

From the grape marbled solid, cut:
- 5 strips, 2" x 42"
- 16 squares, 3" x 3"
- 4 squares, 3⅜" x 3⅜"

From *each* of 4 fat quarters of marbled solid, cut:
- 12 squares, 3" x 3" (48 total)
- 3 squares, 3⅜" x 3⅜" (12 total)

From *each* remaining fat quarter of marbled solid, cut:
- 16 squares, 3" x 3" (64 total)
- 4 squares, 3⅜" x 3⅜" (16 total)

From the *lengthwise* grain of the 1⅝ yards of multicolored geometric print, cut:
- 4 strips, 4" x 58"
- 4 strips, 2" x 58"

From the remaining 1⅝ yards of multicolored geometric print, cut:
- 4 squares, 3⅜" x 3⅜"
- 8 rectangles, 3" x 5½"

From *each* of 4 fat quarters of multicolored geometric print, cut:
- 3 squares, 3⅜" x 3⅜" (12 total)
- 6 rectangles, 3" x 5½" (24 total)

From *each* remaining fat quarter of multicolored geometric print, cut:
- 4 squares, 3⅜" x 3⅜" (16 total)
- 8 rectangles, 3" x 5½" (32 total)

Making the Blocks

Note: *You may find it helpful to presort 32 matching pairs of 3" marbled squares and 3" x 5½" multicolored rectangles.*

1. Using a pencil and ruler, draw a diagonal line from corner to corner on the wrong side of half (64) of the 3" marbled squares. Place a marked square on the right edge of each multicolored 3" x 5½" rectangle, with right sides together and raw edges aligned. Sew directly on the marked line. Trim away the excess fabric, leaving a ¼" seam allowance; press. Make 64, in matching pairs.

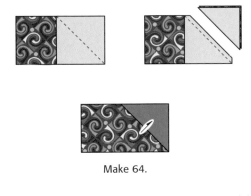

Make 64.

2. Using a pencil and ruler, draw a diagonal line from corner to corner on the wrong side of each 3⅜" marbled square. Duplicating the fabric combinations of the step 1 units, place a marked square on a multicolored 3⅜" square, with right sides together and raw edges aligned. Stitch ¼" on each side of the diagonal line. Cut along the drawn diagonal line to yield two half-square-triangle units; press. Make 64 units in matching pairs, each 3" x 3".

Make 64.

3. Sew matching-colored units from steps 1 and 2 and a matching-colored marbled 3" square together as shown; press. Make 64.

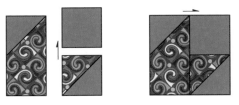

Make 64.

4. Arrange two pairs of matching-colored units from step 3 into rows as shown. Sew the units into rows; press. Sew the rows together to complete the block; press. Make 16 blocks.

Make 16.

Assembling the Quilt Top

1. Arrange and sew the blocks in four rows of four blocks each; press.

2. Sew the rows together; press.

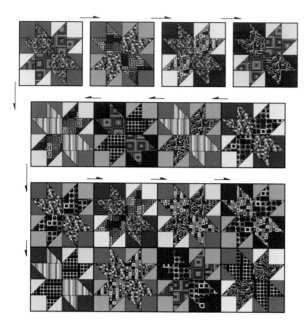

Adding the Borders

For detailed instructions, refer to "Borders with Overlapped Corners" on page 10.

1. Join the inner-border strips end to end to make a continuous strip. Measure the quilt through the center from top to bottom, and cut two border strips to fit that measurement.

2. Sew the trimmed border strips to the side edges of the quilt top. Press toward the border strips.

3. Measure the quilt through the center from side to side, including the borders just added. Cut two border strips to fit that measurement.

4. Sew the trimmed border strips to the top and bottom edges of the quilt top; press.

5. Repeat steps 1–4 to measure, trim, and add the outer-border strips. (You will not need to piece the strips.) Press toward the outer-border strips.

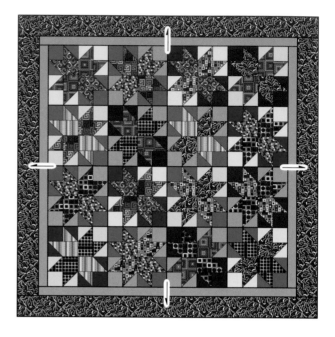

Finishing the Quilt

For detailed instructions on the following finishing techniques, refer to pages 13–17 of "Quiltmaking Basics."

1. Cut and piece the backing fabric so it is 4" to 6" larger than the quilt top. Layer the quilt top, batting, and backing; baste.

2. Hand or machine quilt as desired. Suggestions include machine quilting in the ditch, quilting large circles at the intersection of four marbled solids, and stipple quilting the border.

3. Square up the quilt sandwich.

4. Prepare and sew the binding to the quilt. Add a hanging sleeve, if desired, and a label.

MEMORY GARDEN

By Nancy Mahoney

From the collection of Timeless Treasures, featuring their Country Fair fabrics.

Finished Quilt Size: 38½" x 38½"

Finished Block Size: 10"

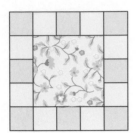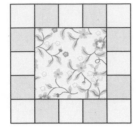

Use this simple block to showcase either a beautiful floral, dignified toile, conversation, or novelty print. With that special fabric and two coordinates—just three fabrics!—you're ready to start stitching. This makes a great choice when you need to whip up a quilt in a hurry for a gift or special occasion. It's so much fun, betcha can't make just one!

Materials

Yardage is based on 42"-wide fabric.

1 yard of yellow floral print for blocks and border

⅞ yard of blue tone-on-tone print for blocks and binding

½ yard of yellow tone-on-tone print for blocks

2⅜ yards of fabric for backing*

42" x 42" piece of batting

* If backing fabric is 42" wide *after* washing, you can use a single width of 1⅜ yards.

Cutting

All measurements include ¼" seam allowances. Cut all strips from the crosswise grain.

From the blue tone-on-tone print, cut:
- 5 strips, 2" x 42"
- 6 strips, 2½" x 42"; crosscut each into 2 strips, 2½" x 21" (12 total)

From the yellow tone-on-tone print, cut:
- 6 strips, 2½" x 42"; crosscut each into 2 strips, 2½" x 21" (12 total)

From the yellow floral print, cut:
- 4 strips, 4½" x 42"
- 2 strips, 6½" x 42"; crosscut into 9 squares, 6½" x 6½"

Making the Blocks

For detailed instructions, refer to "Making Strip Sets" on page 9.

1. Sew three blue 2½" x 21" strips and two yellow 2½" x 21" strips together to make a strip set as shown; press. Make two strip sets. Crosscut each strip set into 2½" segments. Cut 10.

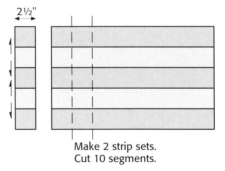

2½"

Make 2 strip sets.
Cut 10 segments.

2. Sew two yellow 2½" x 21" strips and one blue 2½" x 21" strip together to make a strip set as shown; press. Make two strip sets. Crosscut each strip set into 2½" segments. Cut 10.

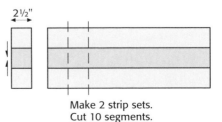

2½"

Make 2 strip sets.
Cut 10 segments.

3. Arrange a yellow floral square and two segments each from steps 1 and 2 as shown. Sew the units together to complete the block; press. Make five blocks and label them block A.

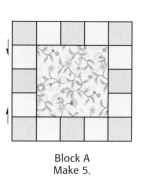
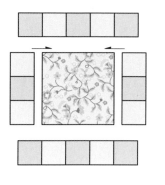

Block A
Make 5.

4. Sew three yellow 2½" x 21" strips and two blue 2½" x 21" strips together to make a strip set as shown; press. Carefully crosscut into eight 2½" segments.

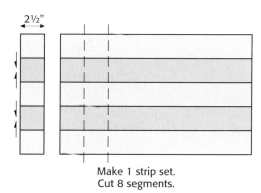

2½"

Make 1 strip set.
Cut 8 segments.

5. Sew two blue 2½" x 21" strips and one yellow 2½" x 21" strip together to make a strip set as shown; press. Carefully crosscut into eight 2½" segments.

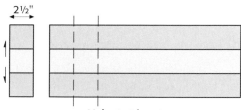

2½"

Make 1 strip set.
Cut 8 segments.

6. Arrange a yellow floral square and two segments each from steps 4 and 5 as shown. Sew the units together to complete the block; press. Make four blocks and label them block B.

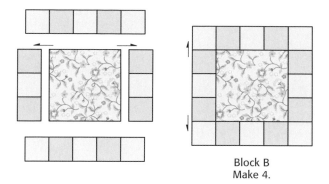

Block B
Make 4.

Assembling the Quilt Top

1. Arrange and sew the blocks in three rows of three blocks each, alternating A and B blocks as shown; press.

2. Sew the rows together; press.

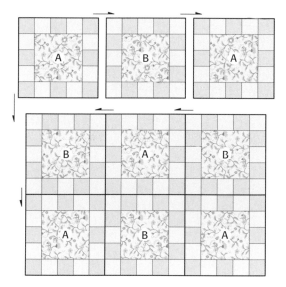

Adding the Borders

For detailed instructions, refer to "Borders with Overlapped Corners" on page 10.

1. Measure the quilt through the center from top to bottom and cut two border strips to fit that measurement.

2. Sew the trimmed border strips to the side edges of the quilt top. Press toward the border strips.

3. Measure the quilt through the center from side to side, including the borders just added. Cut two border strips to fit that measurement.

4. Sew the trimmed border strips to the top and bottom edges of the quilt top; press.

Finishing the Quilt

For detailed instructions on the following finishing techniques, refer to pages 13–17 of "Quiltmaking Basics."

1. If necessary, cut and piece the backing fabric so it is 4" to 6" larger than the quilt top. Layer the quilt top, batting, and backing; baste.

2. Hand or machine quilt as desired. Suggestions include machine quilting in the ditch and quilting the border with a continuous quilting design of small and large loops.

3. Square up the quilt sandwich.

4. Prepare and sew the binding to the quilt. Add a hanging sleeve, if desired, and a label.

Other Options

"Construction Zone" (shown below) illustrates another design option. Combine eight different marbled solids to make the strip sets, and feature a novelty print as the center square of each block. All of the blocks are the same, so make nine of block A only.

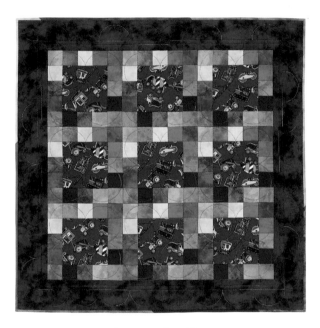

Construction Zone

BUTTERFLY WINDOWS

By Nancy Mahoney

From the collection of Timeless Treasures, featuring their Butterfly fabrics.

Finished Quilt Size: 46½" x 46½"

Finished Block Size: 6"

This simplified version of the traditional Attic Windows block whips together in no time. Narrow sashing adds depth and dimension to this eye-catching design— the perfect showcase for a conversation or theme print.

Materials

Yardage is based on 42"-wide fabric.

1½ yards of blue butterfly print for outer border

⅝ yard *each* of gold and green marbled solids for blocks

⅝ yard of purple marbled solid for sashing and inner border

1 fat quarter of cream butterfly print for blocks

1 fat quarter *each* of rust leaf and green leaf print for blocks

⅜ yard of rust marbled solid for binding

3 yards of fabric for backing

52" x 52" piece of batting

Cutting

All measurements include ¼" seam allowances. Unless otherwise noted, cut all strips from the crosswise grain. Outer (lengthwise) borders are cut long to allow for fabric shrinkage.

From *each* gold and green marbled solid, cut:
- 2 squares, 9" x 9" (4 total)
- 4 strips, 2" x 42"; crosscut into 25 rectangles, 2" x 5" (50 total)

From the cream butterfly print, cut:
- 9 squares, 5" x 5"

From *each* rust leaf and green leaf print, cut:
- 8 squares, 5" x 5" (16 total)

From the purple marbled solid, cut:
- 4 strips, 1½" x 42"; crosscut into 20 rectangles, 1½" x 6½"
- 4 strips, 1½" x 34½"
- 4 strips, 1½" x 42"

From the *lengthwise* grain of the blue butterfly print, cut:
- 4 strips, 5½" x 54"

From the rust marbled solid, cut:
- 5 strips, 2" x 42"

Making the Blocks

For detailed instructions, refer to "Half-Square-Triangle Units" on page 8.

1. Pair each 9" gold square with a 9" green square, right sides facing up. Cut and piece 2¼"-wide bias strips to make four strip sets. Cut the strip sets to make 25 half-square-triangle units, 2" x 2".

Make 4 strip sets.
Cut 25 units.

2. Sew a unit from step 1, a 5" square, a gold rectangle, and a green rectangle into rows as shown; press. Stitch the rows together to complete the block; press. Make 25 blocks.

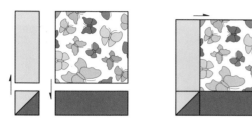

Make 25.

Assembling the Quilt Top

1. Sew five blocks and four purple 1½" x 6½" strips together to make a row; press. Make five rows.

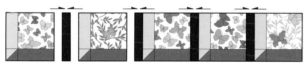

Make 5.

2. Sew the rows of blocks and four purple 1½" x 34½" strips together; press.

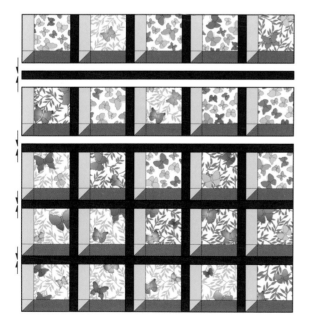

Adding the Borders

For detailed instructions, refer to "Borders with Overlapped Corners" on page 10.

1. Measure the quilt through the center from top to bottom and cut two purple inner-border strips to fit that measurement.

2. Sew the trimmed border strips to the side edges of the quilt top. Press toward the border strips.

3. Measure the quilt from side to side, including the borders just added. Cut two border strips to fit that measurement.

4. Sew the trimmed border strips to the top and bottom edges of the quilt top; press.

5. Repeat steps 1–4 to measure, trim, and add the outer-border strips. Press toward the outer-border strips.

Finishing the Quilt

For detailed instructions on the following finishing techniques, refer to pages 13–17 of "Quiltmaking Basics."

1. Cut and piece the backing fabric so it is 4" to 6" larger than the quilt top. Layer the quilt top, batting, and backing; baste.

2. Hand or machine quilt as desired. Suggestions include machine quilting in the ditch, quilting diagonal lines in the large squares, and stipple quilting the border.

3. Square up the quilt sandwich.

4. Prepare and sew the binding to the quilt. Add a hanging sleeve, if desired, and a label.

BIRD OF PARADISE

By Nancy Mahoney

From the collection of Timeless Treasures, featuring their Paradise fabrics.

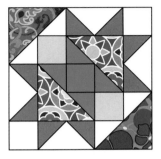

Finished Quilt Size: *60½" x 60½"*

Finished Block Size: *11⅞"*

Don't be intimidated by this intricate-looking design. The Queen's Crown blocks are simple to piece using shortcut techniques. The blocks and bright fabrics combine to create a spectacular quilt with wonderful movement and visual interest.

Materials

Yardage is based on 42"-wide fabric.

2 yards of large-scale floral print for blocks and outer border

1½ yards of cream print for blocks

1 yard of orange print for blocks

⅝ yard of medium-scale floral print for blocks

⅝ yard of green print for blocks

½ yard of blue floral print for blocks

⅜ yard of yellow print for blocks

⅜ yard of blue print for inner border

½ yard of multicolored stripe for binding

4 yards of fabric for backing

65" x 65" piece of batting

Cutting

All measurements include ¼" seam allowances. Unless otherwise noted, cut all strips from the crosswise grain. Outer (lengthwise) borders are cut long to allow for fabric shrinkage.

From the green print, cut:
- 2 strips, 2⅞" x 42"; crosscut into 16 squares, 2⅞" x 2⅞"
- 3 strips, 3¼" x 42"; crosscut into 32 squares, 3¼" x 3¼". Cut once diagonally to yield 64 triangles.

From the yellow print, cut:
- 3 strips, 2⅞" x 42"; crosscut into 32 squares, 2⅞" x 2⅞"

From the medium-scale floral print, cut:
- 3 strips, 5⅝" x 42"; crosscut into 16 squares, 5⅝" x 5⅝". Cut once diagonally to yield 32 triangles.

From the orange print, cut:
- 10 strips, 2⅞" x 42"; crosscut into 128 squares, 2⅞" x 2⅞"

From the cream print, cut:
- 10 strips, 2⅞" x 42"; crosscut into 64 rectangles, 2⅞" x 5¼"
- 3 strips, 3¼" x 42"; crosscut into 32 squares, 3¼" x 3¼". Cut once diagonally to yield 64 triangles.
- 3 strips, 2⅞" x 42"; crosscut into 32 squares, 2⅞" x 2⅞"

From the blue floral print, cut:
- 2 strips, 5⅝" x 42"; crosscut into 8 squares, 5⅝" x 5⅝". Cut once diagonally to yield 16 triangles.

From the *lengthwise* grain of the large-scale floral print, cut:
- 4 strips, 5½" x 72"
- 8 squares, 5⅝" x 5⅝"; cut once diagonally to yield 16 triangles

From the blue print, cut:
- 5 strips, 1¾" x 42"

From the multicolored stripe, cut:
- 7 strips, 2" x 42"

Making the Blocks

1. Sew four green triangles, one green square, and two yellow squares together as shown; press. Add two medium-scale floral triangles; press. Make 16.

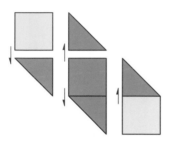

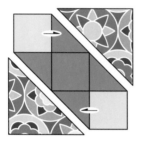

Make 16.

2. Refer to "Making Flying-Geese Units" on page 10. Sew two orange squares to a cream rectangle; press. Make 64.

Make 64.

3. Stitch a unit from step 1, four units from step 2, two cream squares, and four cream triangles together as shown; press. Make 16.

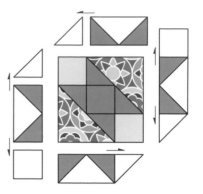

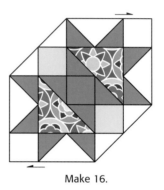

Make 16.

4. Stitch a blue floral triangle and a large-scale floral triangle to each unit from step 3 to complete the block; press. Make 16 blocks.

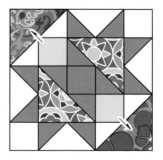

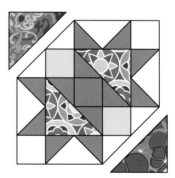

Make 16.

Assembling the Quilt Top

1. Arrange and sew the blocks in four rows of four blocks each, rotating the blocks as shown; press.

2. Sew the rows together; press.

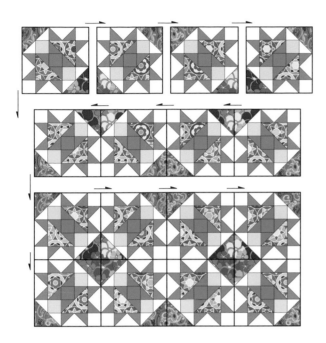

Adding the Borders

For detailed instructions, refer to "Borders with Overlapped Corners" on page 10.

1. Join the inner-border strips end to end to make a continuous strip. Measure the quilt through the center from top to bottom, and cut two border strips to fit that measurement.

2. Sew the trimmed border strips to the side edges of the quilt top. Press toward the border strips.

3. Measure the quilt through the center from side to side, including the borders just added. Cut two border strips to fit that measurement.

4. Sew the trimmed border strips to the top and bottom edges of the quilt top; press.

5. Repeat steps 1–4 to measure, trim, and add the outer-border strips. (You will not need to piece the strips.) Press toward the outer-border strips.

Finishing the Quilt

For detailed instructions on the following finishing techniques, refer to pages 13–17 of "Quiltmaking Basics."

1. Cut and piece the backing fabric so it is 4" to 6" larger than the quilt top. Layer the quilt top, batting, and backing; baste.

2. Hand or machine quilt as desired. Suggestions include machine quilting in the ditch and stipple quilting in the border.

3. Square up the quilt sandwich.

4. Prepare and sew the binding to the quilt. Add a hanging sleeve, if desired, and a label.

GELATO MARMALADE

By Nancy Mahoney

From the collection of Timeless Treasures, featuring their Gelato fabrics.

Finished Quilt Size: 40" x 40"

Finished Block Size: 6"

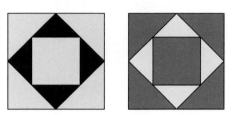

Economy Patch is one of my favorite blocks; it's so versatile and yet so easy to make! This quilt has the complex look we all love in a quilt, but the blocks are small and quick to sew. The warm color palette lends a look of sophistication. As an alternative, you may choose a variety of prints for a more scrappy version.

Materials

Yardage is based on 42"-wide fabric.

1¼ yards of rust marbled print for blocks, outer border, and binding

½ yard of gold marbled print for blocks and inner border

1 fat quarter *each* of 5 light marbled prints for blocks

1 fat quarter *each* of 5 dark marbled prints for blocks

2¾ yards of fabric for backing

44" x 44" piece of batting

Cutting

All measurements include ¼" seam allowances. Unless otherwise noted, cut all strips from the crosswise grain. Outer (lengthwise) borders are cut long to allow for fabric shrinkage.

From the gold marbled print, cut:
- 4 strips, 1½" x 42"
- 2 squares, 3½" x 3½"
- 6 squares, 3" x 3"; cut once diagonally to yield 12 triangles
- 4 squares, 3⅞" x 3⅞"; cut once diagonally to yield 8 triangles

From *each* light marbled-print fat quarter, cut:
- 2 squares, 3½" x 3½" (10 total)
- 4 squares, 3" x 3" (20 total); cut once diagonally to yield 40 triangles
- 4 squares, 3⅞" x 3⅞" (20 total); cut once diagonally to yield 40 triangles

From the *lengthwise* grain of the rust marbled print, cut:
- 4 strips, 4¼" x 45"
- 4 strips, 2" x 45"

From the remaining rust marbled print, cut:
- 3 squares, 3½" x 3½"
- 4 squares, 3" x 3"; cut once diagonally to yield 8 triangles
- 6 squares, 3⅞" x 3⅞"; cut once diagonally to yield 12 triangles

From *each* dark marbled-print fat quarter, cut:
- 2 squares, 3½" x 3½" (10 total)
- 4 squares, 3" x 3" (20 total); cut once diagonally to yield 40 triangles
- 4 squares, 3⅞" x 3⅞" (20 total); cut once diagonally to yield 40 triangles

Making the Blocks

1. Fold a gold or light marbled-print square in half vertically and horizontally, and lightly crease to mark the center of each side. Fold four matching 3" rust or dark marbled-print triangles in

half, and lightly crease to mark the center of the long side. Stitch triangles to opposite sides of the square, matching the center creases; press. Stitch triangles to the remaining sides of the square; press. Make 12 and label them unit A.

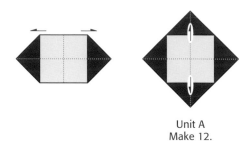

Unit A
Make 12.

2. Repeat step 1, using rust and dark marbled squares and gold and light marbled triangles. Make 13 and label them unit B.

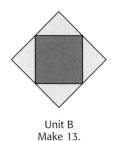

Unit B
Make 13.

3. Fold four matching 3⅞" gold or light marbled-print triangles in half and lightly crease to mark the center of the long side. Stitch triangles to opposite sides of a unit A from step 1, matching the center crease to the crossed seam; press. Stitch triangles to the remaining sides of the square to complete the block; press. Make 12 and label them block A.

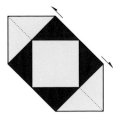

Block A
Make 12.

4. Repeat step 3, using rust and dark marbled triangles and B units from step 2. Make 13 and label them block B.

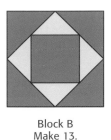

Block B
Make 13.

Assembling the Quilt Top

1. Arrange and sew the blocks in five rows of five blocks each, alternating A and B blocks as shown; press.

2. Sew the rows together; press.

Adding the Borders

For detailed instructions, refer to "Borders with Overlapped Corners" on page 10.

1. Measure the quilt through the center from top to bottom and cut two inner-border strips to fit that measurement.

2. Sew the trimmed border strips to the side edges of the quilt top. Press toward the border strips.

3. Measure the quilt through the center from side to side, including the borders just added. Cut two inner-border strips to fit that measurement.

4. Sew the trimmed border strips to the top and bottom edges of the quilt top; press.

5. Repeat steps 1–4 to measure, trim, and add the outer-border strips. Press toward the outer-border strips.

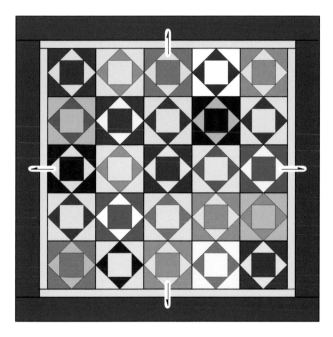

Finishing the Quilt

For detailed instructions on the following finishing techniques, refer to pages 13–17 of "Quiltmaking Basics."

1. Cut and piece the backing fabric so it is 4" to 6" larger than the quilt top. Layer the quilt top, batting, and backing; baste.

2. Hand or machine quilt as desired. Suggestions include machine quilting in the ditch, quilting a circle motif in the center squares, and quilting the border with swirls, loops, and circles.

3. Square up the quilt sandwich.

4. Prepare and sew the binding to the quilt. Add a hanging sleeve, if desired, and a label.

Other Options

"Raspberry Ice" (shown below) illustrates another design option. Each block uses three different fabrics. Block B has a light center square, medium triangles, and dark outer triangles. Block A reverses the order.

Raspberry Ice

STARS OF PROVENCE

By Nancy Mahoney

From the collection of Timeless Treasures, featuring their Provence fabrics.

Finished Quilt Size: 68½" x 68½"

Finished Block Size: 12"

This gorgeous quilt has a timeless, old-fashioned quality, which I achieved by using a large-scale floral print in the setting squares. The Fancy Contrary Wife block may look challenging, but shortcut techniques make construction quite simple. A complementary floral border enhances the look.

Materials

Yardage is based on 42"-wide fabric.

2¼ yards of red floral border stripe for border

1½ yards of red large-scale floral print for setting squares and setting triangles

1⅛ yard of gold paisley for blocks

⅞ yard of green leaf print for blocks and binding

⅝ yard of red small-scale floral print for blocks

⅝ yard of red-and-black floral print for blocks

⅜ yard of gold small-scale floral print for inner border

⅜ yard of green circle print for blocks

⅜ yard of medium-scale floral print for blocks

4¼ yards of fabric for backing

74" x 74" piece of batting

Cutting

All measurements include ¼" seam allowances. Unless otherwise noted, cut all strips from the crosswise grain. Outer (lengthwise) borders are cut long to allow for fabric shrinkage.

From the gold paisley, cut:
- 3 strips, 2½" x 42"; crosscut into 36 squares, 2½" x 2½"
- 1 rectangle, 18" x 21"
- 1 rectangle, 9" x 21"
- 2 strips, 5¼" x 42"; crosscut into 9 squares, 5¼" x 5¼". Cut twice diagonally to yield 36 triangles.

From the red small-scale floral print, cut:
- 1 rectangle, 18" x 21"
- 1 rectangle, 9" x 21"

From the green circle print, cut:
- 3 strips, 2½" x 42"; crosscut into 36 squares, 2½" x 2½"

From the green leaf print, cut:
- 2 strips, 5¼" x 42"; crosscut into 9 squares, 5¼" x 5¼". Cut twice diagonally to yield 36 triangles.
- 8 strips, 2" x 42"

From the red-and-black floral print, cut:
- 3 strips, 5¼" x 42"; crosscut into 18 squares, 5¼" x 5¼". Cut twice diagonally to yield 72 triangles.

From the medium-scale floral print, cut:
- 9 squares, 4½" x 4½"

From the red large-scale floral print, cut:
- 4 squares, 12½" x 12½"
- 2 squares, 18¼" x 18¼"; cut twice diagonally to yield 8 side setting triangles
- 2 squares, 9⅜" x 9⅜"; cut once diagonally to yield 4 corner setting triangles

From the gold small-scale floral print, cut:
- 6 strips, 1½" x 42"

From the *lengthwise* grain of the red floral border stripe, cut:

❖ 4 strips, 8" x 81"*

* *Border width may vary, depending upon the width of the stripe you choose. Be sure to add ½" to the finished width for seam allowances.*

Making the Blocks

For detailed instructions, refer to "Half-Square-Triangle Units" on page 8.

1. Pair the gold paisley and red small-scale floral 9" x 21" rectangles, and the gold paisley and red small-scale floral 18" x 21" rectangles, right sides facing up. Cut and piece 2½"-wide bias strips to make four strip sets. Cut the strip sets to make 72 half-square-triangle units, 2½" x 2½".

Make 4 strip sets.
Cut 72 units.

2. Sew a gold paisley square, a green circle print square, and two units from step 1 into rows as shown; press. Sew the rows together; press. Make 36.

Make 36.

3. Sew each green leaf triangle to a red-and-black triangle; press. Make 36. Sew each gold paisley triangle to a red-and-black triangle; press. Make 36. Sew the triangle units together; press. Make 36.

Make 36.

4. Sew a medium-scale floral square, four units from step 2, and four units from step 3 into rows as shown; press. Sew the rows together to complete the block; press. Make nine blocks.

Make 9.

Assembling the Quilt Top

1. Arrange the blocks, red large-scale floral squares, and corner and side setting triangles in diagonal rows as shown.

2. Sew the blocks, squares, and triangles together in diagonal rows; press.

3. Sew the rows together. Press the seams in one direction.

Adding the Borders

For detailed instructions, refer to "Borders with Overlapped Corners" on page 10 and "Borders with Mitered Corners" also on page 10.

1. Join the inner-border strips end to end to make a continuous strip. Measure the quilt through the center from top to bottom and cut two border strips to fit that measurement.

2. Sew the trimmed border strips to the side edges of the quilt top. Press toward the border strips.

3. Measure the quilt through the center from side to side, including the borders just added. Cut two border strips to fit that measurement.

4. Sew the trimmed border strips to the top and bottom edges of the quilt top; press.

5. Measure, trim, and sew the outer-border strips to the quilt, mitering the corners. Press toward the border strips.

Finishing the Quilt

For detailed instructions on the following finishing techniques, refer to pages 13–17 of "Quiltmaking Basics."

1. Cut and piece the backing fabric so it is 4" to 6" larger than the quilt top. Layer the quilt top, batting, and backing; baste.

2. Hand or machine quilt as desired. Suggestions include machine quilting in the ditch and quilting the border by following the lines in the border fabric.

3. Square up the quilt sandwich.

4. Prepare and sew the binding to the quilt. Add a hanging sleeve, if desired, and a label.

ABOUT THE AUTHOR

Nancy Mahoney is an enthusiastic quiltmaker, teacher, fabric designer, and author. She enjoys speaking at quilt guilds and meeting other quilters, especially beginners. She also enjoys creating traditional quilts that look complex but are easy to make. This is her third book with Martingale & Company.

Nancy began actively quilting in 1987, after taking a scrap-quilt class from Marsha McCloskey. Nancy's quilt from that class appears in the book *A Dozen Variables* by Marsha McCloskey and Nancy J. Martin. Nancy's quilts have also been featured in many other quilt books as well as in a number of national quilt magazines. Through the years her quilts have won many awards, including two first-place ribbons. She enjoys the art of quiltmaking and believes that each quilt is an exciting learning experience. For Nancy, making beautiful quilts is fun!

Nancy lives in Palm Coast, Florida. When she's not quilting, she enjoys gardening, walking on the beach, and shopping for antiques.